VOICE FROM CONAKRY

VOICE FROM CONAKRY

Kwame Nkrumah

Panaf Books

Voice from Conakry

© Panaf Books

First published in 1967
Reprinted 1969, 1971, 1973, 1980, 2006

ISBN: 0 901787 02 7

Panaf Books
75 Weston Street
London SE1 3RS

INTRODUCTION

These broadcasts to the people of Ghana were made in Conakry between March and December 1966 on Radio Guinea's "Voice of the Revolution". Their purpose was first, to expose the true nature of the so-called coup carried out on 24th February 1966 by traitors among the Army and Police inspired and aided by local reactionaries, imperialists and neo-colonialists; and secondly, to encourage resistance.

When the broadcasts were made, the people of Ghana were being subjected to oppressive decrees and to campaigns of vile propaganda and lies designed to destroy my image, and to justify the abandonment of all our hard-won socialist gains and achievements. They were told that the country was on the verge of bankruptcy and that a massive sell-out to foreign capitalists was the only solution.

Similar lies were spread throughout the world by the capitalist-imperialist press, with unprecedented dishonesty and ferocity, in books, magazines and newspapers.

The traitors struck in February 1966, shortly after the inauguration of the Volta Dam, just as we were on the point of break-through in our struggle to achieve economic independence. In doing so, they betrayed not only Ghanaians, but millions of poor and oppressed people in Africa and elsewhere who looked to Ghana for inspiration and leadership.

I was determined in my broadcasts to expose the counter-revolutionary nature of the "coup", and at the same time to show how the blow struck against progressive Ghana was also an attempt to set back the pace of the wider African Revolution for total liberation and an All-African Government.

The gallant stand of members of the Presidential Guard Regiment at Flagstaff House on 24th February 1966 was symbolic of the courage and determined resistance shown by the people of Ghana to the puppet "NLC" right from the start. Widespread resistance, both open and underground, has continued and increased ever since. If my broadcasts contributed in any way to stimulate the political awareness of Ghanaians at home and abroad and to stiffen their determination to overthrow the traitorous "NLC", I consider they served their purpose.

Kwame Nkrumah

Conakry
1 May 1967

VOICE FROM CONAKRY

1. I expect you all at this hour of trial to remain firm in determination and resistance despite intimidation.

6th March 1966

FELLOW countrymen, Chiefs and people, I am speaking to you from Radio Guinea, Conakry. On the eve of the 6th of March, Ghana's Independence Day, I send to you all, greetings and warm regards.

It was on this day that the combined forces of the Ghana people secured Independence from British imperialism. This achievement was not an easy task. It involved sacrifice, suffering and deprivation on the part of all of us.

It was only when I arrived at Peking in China that I was informed that some members of my Armed Forces, supported by some members of my Police had attempted to overthrow my Government. I know that you are always loyal to me, the Party and the Government and I expect you all at this hour of trial to remain firm in determination and resistance despite intimidation.

The people of Ghana built up the Convention People's Party which became the vanguard of the national liberation movement in Ghana. By indomitable will the Convention People's Party overcame all difficulties, triumphed over adversities and won independence and planned for the economic, political and social construction of our dear Ghana. The Party and Government fought not only for political independence but evolved a work and happiness programme of reconstruction. We also joined in the great movement for the liberation and political unification of Africa.

The achievement of the Convention People's Party under my leadership is an open book. It can be seen by all, and today, anyone who visits Ghana can be a witness of this great achievement. Internationally, independent Ghana has been playing her role in world affairs. She has supported peace

1

and will always continue to support any movement that can lead to the peace and security of the world.

In all this struggle, the Convention People's Party, and its Government have not shed a single drop of a Ghanaian's blood. I shuddered when I learnt of the shooting and killing of defenceless men and women, and the arrest, intimidation and imprisonment of many of the leading patriots of the country. The blood of these gallant men and women cry to heaven for redress. Their blood shall not be shed in vain. Those who have died, may they rest in peace.

By the arrest, detention and assassination of Ministers, the Party's civil servants, trade unionists and by the blind massacre of defenceless men and women, the authors of these insane acts of robbery, violence, intimidation and assassination have added brutality to their treason.

Never before in the cherished history of our new Ghana have citizens, men and women, been assassinated in cold blood; and never have their children become orphans for political reasons. Never before have Ghanaians been shot down because of their political convictions. This is a tragedy of monstrous proportions.

But I know your courage and determination: I see the extent of your indignation against this wanton rebellion. I know that at the appropriate time you will take the initiative to crush it. The Party's dynamism will rise up again to save your dignity and personality. As far as I am concerned I will do my very best to crush this criminal rebellion.

The integral wings of the Convention People's Party, the Farmers Co-operative Council, the Trades Union Congress, the National Council of Ghana Women, the Young Pioneers, the Workers' Brigade have been established by the Party and the spirit that motivates these organisations cannot be destroyed. They now suffer in silence but they will rise up again and speak. The present rebellion has not only committed treason against the sovereign state of Ghana but has attacked the very foundation upon which our culture was based—the position of Chieftaincy which has been irrevocably enshrined in our Constitution.

In the Party's struggle for independence we have had opponents and enemies. Imperialism and neo-colonialism and their agents and stooges have not been our friends. They have tried in many ways to undo what the Convention People's Party has done. In all attempts they failed; and even several attempts on my personal life have failed. And so, if today we celebrate our 9th Anniversary of Independence, we have a lot to be thankful for.

Experience has given us added wisdom to continue the struggle. No one can destroy the socialist gains we have achieved. For no reason other than morbid ambition, inordinate and selfish desire for power, certain officers of my Armed Forces took advantage of my absence from Accra to subvert and rebel against constitutional authority. This reactionary rebellion sought to perpetrate subversive activities against the lawfully constituted Government of Ghana.

What has taken place in Ghana is not a coup d'état but a rebellion and it shall be crushed by its own actions. At the moment you are being suppressed at the point of guns and bayonets and you are made speechless by these same instruments. You are forbidden to hold your rallies and meetings. But, I know that even in silence you are determined and resisting. Be assured that I am standing firm behind you. There is a Russian proverb which says that one cannot screen the sun by the palm of a hand; nor can I be destroyed by telling lies about me. Very soon I shall be with you again.

The perpetrators of this rebellion have committed an act of high treason. Those soldiers of my army who have taken power in my absence have issued orders that our 9th Anniversary of Independence, a great national day, should not be celebrated. This shows that they are suppressing you at the points of guns and bayonets. They cannot destroy what we have taken years to build. For, what we have achieved is built on rock foundations and is indestructible. Forward Ever, Backward Never. There is Victory for Us.

I am safe and well. I will be with you in due course. Have courage and bear your humiliation and sufferings with fortitude. What has happened is only a phase of our struggle and it shall pass.

> Long live the people of Ghana
> Long live the Convention People's Party
> Long live the liberation movement of Africa
> Long live the African continental government that must be

2. Ghana is out of the gambling house of colonialism and will never return to it again.

13th March 1966

CHIEFS and people, men and women of Ghana, the rank and file of the Convention People's Party, once again I speak to you from Conakry on Radio Guinea's "Voice of the Revolution."

A week ago I spoke to you on the day of the 9th Anniversary of our Independence. Since then I have learnt, with some amusement, of the feeble attempts by the so-called National Liberation Council to prevent you from using your own wireless sets for fear you might hear my voice. Perhaps they are unaware that the desire of the masses cannot be denied nor their will thwarted. You may cow them with tommy-guns and bayonets for a time but not the whole time.

Countrymen, I am sure you already realise that this so-called Council does not constitute a new government of Ghana in Accra. What you find in Accra now is no more than a clique of military and police adventurers who are attempting to destroy and set back the economic, political and social gains of the people of Ghana. In this nefarious pursuit they are being propelled by neo-colonialists and their agents who have resorted to the use of force to keep the people of Ghana oppressed. But they will fail. Indeed, they have failed. As I told you in my last broadcast, the Convention People's Party is still the vanguard of the People's political movement, and I am still the constitutional head of the Ghana State.

I am sure that even those army and police adventurers and traitors know that without the support of the masses they have no existence. They also know that the people of Ghana are behind me. Hence, the vicious propaganda and vilifications they are spreading about my government and the Convention People's Party and its integral wings.

These people have underestimated the strength of the masses; they have miscalculated the dynamic force of the Convention People's Party. Before your united might, confronted with your mass strength, the wall of bayonets and rifles and tommy-guns they have erected around you will collapse. I know you will rise up in your mass strength, to

4

break through it and overthrow these irresponsible army and police traitors and adventurers.

I am sure that already in their hearts these enemies of the people regret the folly of their action and go in daily fear of its consequences, for they feel your anger like the Sword of Damocles hanging over their heads. Not even their neo-colonialist and imperialist backers can save them from your wrath when you rise again.

It was the late Major-General Barwah who in his humble and amiable frank way told me that the Ghana Army could not take political power and exist in Ghana. As I promised you in my last broadcast I shall be with you very soon and I am confident that you shall prove him right. First, stand firm in your determination, even though you suffer in silence, and resist all terrorism and buccaneering, martial law and false propaganda, with moral stamina and spiritual fortitude. The physical resistance will emerge by itself.

But, what has made these army and police officers take the step that they have taken, and why did they do so during my absence from Ghana?

If they felt strong and confident in themselves why did they make this treacherous move only when I was away? They thought that supported by their imperialist and neo-colonialist masters, they could terrorise you into subjugation, with rifles, bayonets, and tommy-guns, and force anarchy and destruction on you. They chose my absence as the most opportune time for their treachery because they dared not do it in my presence. They have bitten more than they can swallow and their days of reckoning are approaching.

As for the imperialists and neo-colonialists, they have only succeeded in aiding and abetting the insane murderers of patriotic citizens in cold blood, and the killers of innocent loyal army officers. The stand of neo-colonialism in Africa is being challenged by us and very soon it too will collapse.

The anarchy and terrorism these mutineers and traitors have tried to establish in Ghana cannot last very long. It is bound to be of short duration, and as I last assured you, it shall soon pass away. Then, you will find yourselves reborn in a strength which was previously not experienced by the people of Ghana.

I know that the bulk of the army and police does not sup-

5

port this rebellious clique. In fact I know, that, but for the treacherous instigation of certain police officers with neo-colonialist bias, my armed forces would have thought twice before stooping to such a disgraceful act of rebellion for which there is no reason whatsoever. It is sheer stupidity and vandalism. I know, that there are many in my armed forces who are loyal to me and even though they are either being misguided, intimidated or bullied now, they will rise again with the people to defend the people's cause. I should know this, because the Ghana Armed Forces is my own creation. I reorganised the Army myself, founded the Ghana Air Force, and established the Navy from scratch. I remember it was only very recently that I ordered seven jet fighters from Italy for the Air Force for training purposes. Unfortunately, two crashed and Ghana is now left with five.

Countrymen, when you see these traitorous rebels strutting around the Accra streets looking pretentiously menacing, when you are continuously disturbed by the whines of the five jet fighters as they engage in aerobatics over the city of Accra, do not be afraid or be cowed. For, as the creator of the Ghana Armed Forces, I assure you that even their combined strength is powerless and harmless. An eloquent testimony of their weakness is borne by the great resistance they encountered from the handful of my Guard Regiment at Flagstaff House.

Perhaps we owe a lot to the Ghanaian's inherent love for peace, because due to this peaceful disposition we did not build our Armed Forces for external defence. We only maintained a token force for internal security. For the same reason the Ghana Police Service is unarmed unlike the colonial Police Force. Herein lies the wisdom in late Major-General Barwah's contention that the Ghana Armed Forces can never successfully subjugate the masses. In numbers alone, even the strength of the Workers' Brigade completely overshadows the Armed Forces, and you should draw encouragement and conviction of your strength from the fact that these traitorous rebels have not dared to disband the Workers' Brigade, for fear of its strength.

Major-General Barwah's loyalty was unquestioned and the facts of his cold-blooded murder make a classic example of cowardly assassination. You know how he was awakened in the small hours of the morning by some of the rebel army officers, and how they shot him dead at close range because he flatly and categorically refused to join the plot and hand the army to them. These cowards cannot wash his blood off their hands by turning round to give him a military funeral. He is dead, but I know that as Chief of Army Staff, there are some army officers who are still loyal to him and these will rise and avenge his death at the right time, even though now they suffer in silence.

Countrymen, at this time of trial, it is important that you maintain your silent resistance. Be confident, and very soon you will rise again to put these imperialist and neo-colonialist inspired rebels and adventurers in their correct places. The will of the broad masses of the people of Ghana will reassert itself. They are forcing you with bayonets and tommy-guns to do as they would like you to do. But intimidation and terrorism will pass away.

It is interesting and at the same time ridiculous, that this clique of army and police adventurers should call themselves a "National Liberation Council." What have they liberated, and what are they trying to liberate? Or do they imagine that they are liberating Ghana in order to make her a present to their imperialist and neo-colonialist masters? I would advise this clique of lying traitors rather to liberate themselves from their neo-colonialist and imperialist masters. Since the 24th February incident, you only have to look around to see the influx into Ghana of these imperialists and neo-colonialists as well as their agents! They stream into the country because they smell a fertile ground for economic subjugation and financial profiteering. This clique of traitors and rebels who are doing so much to prepare the ground for them to come into Ghana must call themselves a Council of Oppression and sell-outs. They are not a National Liberation Council but a Notorious Liars Council.

I know they have told you and are still telling you a lot of lies in an attempt to deceive and mislead you. But take heart, stand firm and oppose their lies and vilifications. The freedom which the people of Ghana under the leadership of the dynamic Convention People's Party fought for and won cannot be destroyed or even set back. Ghana is out of the gambling house of colonialism and will never return to it again. Our secular and religious freedom cannot be destroyed. The forces of light will eventually overcome those of darkness, and truth will always prevail over falsehood. This is a moral law which cannot be denied even if these oppressive rebels and mutineers take your wireless sets away from you or forbid you to use them, by military decrees.

Look at the very composition of the rebel Council, and you will find that it seeks to revive tribalism which we have taken so many years of hard work to eliminate. I assure you that they cannot destroy the socialist gains of the Convention People's Party, or the social state we have created. The same Ghanaian masses who defeated colonialism will also defeat neo-colonialism and their agents in Ghana.

Chiefs and people, men and women of Ghana, this is your hour of trial but we shall triumph over our enemies. I call upon the rank and file of the Convention People's Party, those brave men who won so gallantly against the colonialists in pre-Independence days; I call upon the Farmers Council Co-operatives, the National Council of Ghana Women, the Ghana Moslems' Council, the Workers' Brigade and all Party wings and activists in the nine regions of Ghana, and last but not least, the Young Pioneer Movement and all the youth of Ghana to stand firm in this hour of trial, resist all falsehood and deception, and prepare to revolt against this clique of oppressive and deceiving adventurers. I also call upon those loyal sections of my armed forces and police to identify themselves with the masses and fight at their side to destroy these rebellious traitors and stooges of colonialism. I will personally be with you, and when the time comes you cannot fail to see it. We shall overcome oppression and rebellion. We shall remove the obstacles they seek to place in the path of Ghana's progress; and peace will come again to our beloved Ghana, cleansing it of the vilifications, shame and abuses which these adventurers and mutineers and their imperialist and neo-colonialist masters have tried to heap upon Ghana.

There is victory for us. Our battle cry must be "Away with the stooges of neo-colonialism. Away with Imperialism. Down with the clique of Army and Police adventurers. Onward to social, economic and political progress of the fatherland. Forward, to the glory of Ghana and Africa. Long live the Convention People's Party. Long live the African Revolution."

3. The instigated rebellion by certain army and police officers in Ghana was directed not only against Ghana, but also against the African Revolution and the unity and independence of our continent.

20th March 1966

FELLOW countrymen of Ghana, once again I speak to you from the "Voice of the Revolution," Radio Guinea, Conakry.

It is not insignificant that the "Voice of the Revolution" should be the medium through which I speak to you. The instigated rebellion by certain army and police officers in Ghana was directed not only against Ghana but also against the African Revolution and the unity and independence of our continent. They hoped, through such irresponsible action to strangle Ghana and undermine the African Revolution.

For years I have been talking and speaking, writing and teaching about imperialism, colonialism and neo-colonialism in order to create an awareness of their workings and machinations. Only a sell-out willing tool, a quisling and a lackey, a stooge and a traitor could fall victim to the wiles of imperialism, colonialism and neo-colonialism. The pity is that there are still Ghanaians and Africans who are prepared to sell themselves to aid and abet these systems.

These agents and stooges chose to attack the African Revolution by attacking me. They know, that the name of Ghana is one of the symbols of African achievement. It was so in medieval Africa, and it is so today. The re-awakened African giant is the master-organ for African progress, national consciousness and African unity. It is the symbol of the courageous struggle of the African people for national independence and continental unity.

From pre-independence days to the day we fought for and won our independence from colonial rule—the symbolic date being 6th March 1957—Ghana has thrown herself freely and boldly into the struggle for African emancipation. We have proclaimed our firm stand against imperialism, colonialism and neo-colonialism. We have unflinchingly stated that the independence of Ghana was meaningless unless it was linked up with the total liberation of the African continent. We

9

made it clear to our brother African States which followed us in the wake of African freedom and independence that unless Africa was politically united our continent would never be really free from foreign interference and domination. We also warned that imperialism and neo-colonialism would turn some of us into stooges and traitors in order to undermine and subvert not only the African Revolution but the very existence of independent African states. This has become our cardinal foreign policy and this is what we have been shouting from roof-tops all over the African continent. The African freedom fighters joined us in the struggle and we welcomed them as worthy sons and daughters of Africa who shared our hopes for a United Revolutionary Africa. Thanks to the efforts of African freedom fighters and revolutionaries, today there are no fewer than 36 Independent African States united under the banner of the Organisation of African Unity. The Organisation of African Unity presents a common front in the struggle to free and unite Africa and claim for her the international recognition, dignity and respect which is Africa's due.

Ghana and the Convention People's Party have never been forgiven by their enemies for their firm stand and the part they play in the African revolutionary struggle for emancipation and unity. Since independence they have tried various strategems to overthrow Ghana and make her subservient to their whims and caprices. Our firm policy of positive neutralism and non-alignment thwarts their plans and baulks their policy of undermining us.

In public education, public health and social development Ghana today is as example of success. Thanks to the workers, farmers and peasants of Ghana the standard of living in Ghana today is one of the highest in Africa. What we have achieved belongs to the people and not to a clique of self-seeking people, or a class. The people themselves know this.

This unwarranted rebellion threatens to destroy all that the Ghanaian people hold dear to heart. This senseless rebellion threatens the achievements we have sweated for, for the past 15 restless years. By this rebellion, they have tried to set back what we have achieved. They have attacked Ghana and the African Revolution but they cannot succeed. We will not allow them to succeed. These stooges and sycophants of neo-colonialism may temporarily set-back Ghana's progress, and impede the African political movement for a time. They may destroy some of our work of patience, diligence and sacrifice but we will rebuild what they destroy. Our socialist gains and achievements can never be destroyed.

It is only unfortunate that for Ghana, the various projects and factories which were started by my government have all been abandoned by this so-called National Liberation Council.

The Seven-Year Development Plan has also been abandoned by this treacherous clique whose members are too ignorant to realise that a planted seed takes time to germinate before sprouting into the glorious foliage that is visible to all. All the projects which would have benefited us in future have been abandoned. Where does Ghana stand now? It means we stand on the verge of chaos and confusion.

It is also sad that for Africa, the movement to liberate our oppressed brothers of Zimbabwe will be temporarily weakened and our drive for African continental political unity slowed down.

Countrymen, the actions of this clique of army and police renegades has put us one step backward, but we shall take two steps forward. Stand firm and have confidence in the Convention People's Party and victory will be ours. We have beaten them before; and we shall beat them again.

Fellow countrymen, say nothing if this or that country recognises this rebellious clique. The recognition or non-recognition of this traitorous clique is irrelevant to the situation. The struggle is a revolutionary struggle. Remember that the struggle of Ghana and Africa has only reached a new phase —a stage of rebirth out of which shall emerge a greater consciousness of the African personality and dignity. We must evolve new forms of revolutionary struggle to meet the new African situation.

Countrymen, as I speak to you now, several ships that should have unloaded their cargoes of materials and machinery meant for Ghana's industries and factories at Tema harbour, have all returned to their home bases because of the actions of these traitorous rebels. They were not allowed to unload these cargoes at Tema. I shall be with you sooner than our detractors expect and we shall again take up the reins of our industrial development.

I have been told of the diabolical acts of brutality, assassination and barbarism which this murderous army and police rebels have been perpetrating against the people of Ghana. The number of defenceless men and women who have been beaten up, murdered or maimed is simply heart-breaking. Misled soldiers and police break into people's homes heartlessly machine-gun their occupants, to come out not only with dead bodies but carrying refrigerators, wireless sets, boxes or portmanteaus and other personal belongings of their victims. Mothers are murdered in their own homes. With appalling barbarism their children are snatched from their lifeless embrace and flung from third and second-floor windows to crash dead on concrete pavements below. Countrymen, these sad facts speak of hideous acts which one never thought could be perpetrated by any persons who call themselves Ghanaians. This lunatic fringe of the army and police, a relic of our colonial heritage, should not escape the blame and responsibility for these crimes. They will not go unpunished.

Since the 24th February incident crimes ranging from looting, maltreatment, torture and massacre of defenceless citizens have become the order of the day in Accra and other regions of Ghana. This clique of rebels have suppressed all fundamental liberties which were ours under our constitution. They have forbidden the holding of meetings and rallies, people are not allowed to use their own wireless sets; cabinet members, leading civil servants and public servants, responsible men in Ghanaian society, able heads and directors of state corporations and state enterprises have all been thrown ignominiously into prison; the masses are tortured and humiliated. African freedom fighters in training at Accra and African political refugees have been shamelessly molested and heartlessly carted away at gun-point to some bizarre fate at the hands of those from whom they sought to escape.

These are sad facts facing Ghana now, and their perpetrators brazenly call themselves a national liberation council. What do these hirelings and murderers know about national liberation? Where were they when we were fighting to liberate the then Gold Coast from the clutches of the imperialist and colonialist exploiters? Countrymen, these villains were in the country at the time but wherever and whenever they appeared

12

they traitorously backed the colonial oppressors with whom they have always had a common interest.

Today they clumsily lie that they are national liberators and by force of arms they seek to abolish the constitution established according to the will of the majority of the Ghanaian people. By force of arms they seek to abolish the people's elected parliament. By force of arms they seek to dissolve the people's chosen party, the Convention People's Party. Indeed, by force of arms, they seek to abolish or dissolve all forms of democracy in Ghana! What are their intentions? What are they after? They seek no more than their own selfish interests—interests which are based on the systematic forceful suppression of the Ghanaian masses. Such is the evil content of this murderous rebellion.

They have surrounded you not only with guns and bayonets but also with lies and calumny, in an attempt to throw dust into your eyes and blind you to the true, evil content of their treachery. But I know they cannot deceive you with the lies they have fabricated against me and my government, such as the nonsensical talk about the breaking down of Ghana's economy and the nonsense about Kwame Nkrumah's property. It is common knowledge—and the army and police rebels know this—that Kwame Nkrumah has no personal property and that all that he has belongs to the Party and the State.

This clique of army and police traitors have brazenly challenged the constitutional authority of the state and are attempting to destroy our socialist gains and achievements. There were no grounds whatsover for this murderous rebellion. And now that they know they have misfired they seek to fabricate lies to justify their treachery and employ torture and intimidation to force and coerce loyal citizens into submission. They make false statements and publish false news about innocent and loyal citizens whom they hold at the points of guns and bayonets. Ministers and important members of the community have been illegally thrown into prison and they have even established "Committees of Enquiry" to aid them in their fabrications. However, no amount of lies and calumny can justify their groundless and murderous actions or absolve them from the punishment which they deserve.

Workers, farmers and peasants of Ghana, militant men and

women of the Convention People's Party, Ghana youth in the cities, towns and villages, this is your time to march into double action. We must crush this clique of army and police gangsters who have thrown such dangerous spanners not only into the spokes of the wheels of Ghana's progress and development but also into those of the African revolution. More than ever before the struggle for African emancipation must be intensified. We must overthrow these adventurers and self-seekers with all the means at our command. I shall be with you very soon, and we shall together carry on the revolutionary struggle to its successful conclusion with new spirit and reborn energy. Do not despair; we are not alone in this revolutionary struggle against the enemies of progress and freedom. Hundreds of letters, telegrams and cablegrams condemning the rebellion reach me daily from nationalists and freedom fighters all over Africa and from progressive forces and movements all over the world. I know how you are suffering humiliation and torture in silence now but I know that all of you, men and women and youth are inwardly resisting and at the clarion call which will soon be sounded, you will rise up to fight and conquer this notorious clique of army and police traitors.

I know your courage and determination and I have no doubt that you will join hands in this new struggle to throw out of Ghana these shameful traitors of the nation.

Countrymen, as I have been telling you, do not be deterred or frightened by the rifles and tommy-guns which these traitors intimidate you with. They know they are powerless before your united strength. If we could fight and defeat colonialism how much less is the task of defeating a clique of army and police racketeers who have not got the full support of the whole army and police? This clique is only a section of the army and police who are using tommy-guns and rifles to intimidate, coerce and suppress you. Even among the murderous traitors themselves there is division. Already the conflict between the army rebels and the police traitors is obvious and deepens more and more as they attempt to share the booty and bribes they have gathered from their treachery.

But for disastrous consequences to our economy we would patiently wait for these ignorant rebels to be consumed in

14

the heat of their own follies. If we chose to allow them to exist for some time they would soon crack-up by their own inability, stupidity and mismanagement. But, love of country demands that we crush them quickly before they play too much havoc with our dear Ghana and create confusion within the African revolution. And so, countrymen, let all true Ghanaians remain firm and resistant; let all loyal members of the army and police remain firm wherever they may be. I congratulate the Presidential Guard Regiment for their bold stand at Flagstaff House. Let them also stand firm. We will remember those who are dead.

I know your patriotism and I know that you will continue to fight for and safeguard the dignity, freedom and honour which we owe to Ghana, Africa and the world. Forward ever, Backward never. There is victory for us.

> Long live the Convention People's Party
> Long live the Organisation of African Unity
> Long live the African revolutionary struggle

4. Remain firm, be steadfastly resistant and be prepared.

24th March 1966

FELLOW countrymen, Chiefs and people of Ghana, today, the 24th of March 1966, I wish to speak to you briefly from the "Voice of the Revolution," Radio Guinea, Conakry.

It is exactly one month today since a wanton and unwarranted rebellion by a section of our Army and police took place in Ghana. With this month's passage I am sure that you have now torn off the veil which these reactionary and irresponsible army and police rebels tried to pull over your face through falsehood, lies and intimidation backed by tommy-guns, rifles and bayonets. You can well now realise their treachery in its true and correct perspective. You are beginning to question the reasonability of this rebellion. Your "whys" and "wherefores" may run into hundreds without any satisfactory answers.

Countrymen, this is because nobody can give any convincing reasons why this reactionary army and police clique did what they have done. Convincing reasons simply do not exist as is evidenced by Ghana's achievements and successes under the leadership of the Convention People's Party within at least the last ten years. In fact, these rebels themselves are beginning to realise the folly and unreasonableness of their own action. The progressive world is also wondering and asking for how long are the Chiefs and people, men and women, farmers, workers and peasants of Ghana going to tolerate this obvious treachery and anarchy? For how long are they going to suffer this unbearable humiliation which has been brought upon their heads by this reactionary clique of army and police adventurers?

Countrymen, by now you have torn the veil from your face. It is time for you to act and restore your freedom which has been suddenly taken away from you by this shameless clique. I know that for the past month you have not been able to speak your minds because bayonets and guns are being pointed at you. They have struck fear into you. The attack upon your freedom and liberty was so treacherously done that it took all of you by surprise.

Everything is now clear to you. A month of reflection

should give you the courage to come out in your thousands to crush this rebellion. This is the time to organise yourselves against their treachery. I know you are taking time to sort things out. I have faith in your patience and diligence but these army and police criminals should not be allowed to get away with their crimes against the people of Ghana, the state and the nation. These army and police criminals have brought shame and disgrace upon Ghana and it is your duty to wipe off this disgrace. Act now: the ways to crush them are many and your mass strength is invincible.

The rebellion now looks so stupid and ridiculous in the eyes of the world. For no reason at all, untold hardships, misery and suffering have been brought on the great majority of Ghanaian people by this rebellious act of treason. Imagine the number of people—including army and police officers who refused to take part in this rebellion—who have been murdered in cold blood. Thousands of Party members and Party activists have been detained unlawfully. Ministers, Members of Parliament, Regional and District Commissioners, Party Secretaries, professional men and women have also been detained unlawfully; many of them murdered. University students and professors have been thrown into prison for demonstrating against this clique of neo-colonialist and fascist agents. All the ministers of my government are illegally imprisoned and are being maltreated, tormented and even doped to say things which otherwise they would never dream of saying.

By this rebellion several business firms may be closed down and some private firms may even withdraw their contracts because of the intolerable situation which faces them now in Ghana. Already many professional men and women have left the country, others have been expelled. Ghana's development definitely will come to a standstill.

Countrymen, these are only a few of the monstrous crimes and misdeeds that these army and police rebels and traitors have treacherously committed against Ghana.

They now try to hide their crimes from you through a multiplicity of lies and false propaganda, bribery and corruption. They intimidate and coerce responsible citizens they hold in prison and force them to make false statements and tell untrue stories at gun point.

17

What is the meaning of all the missions which the so-called National Liberation Council is sending out? Why this feverish attempt to send missions abroad, anyway? In fact, if they were sure of their position in Ghana and the world they would not be acting diplomatically so childishly.

Countrymen, as I have always enjoined you, remain firm, be steadfastly resistant and be prepared, for the hour of action draws near. I shall be with you again and we shall together rebuild those parts of our socialist achievements and developments which these traitors and neo-colonialist agents have destroyed. Let the coming months have a story to tell.

> Sons and daughters of Ghana arise and fight
> In the name of the great C.P.P.
> We shall fight and conquer now
> Forward ever, Backward never,
> In the name of the great C.P.P.
> There is victory for us.
> Remember our battle cry is:
> Away with the stooges of neo-colonialism
> Down with the clique of army and police adventurers and reactionaries
> Forward! Progressive workers, Farmers and peasants of Ghana
> Onward to social, economic and political progress of the fatherland
> Long live the Convention People's Party
> Long live the African revolutionary struggle

5. Africa is not dismayed by the events which have taken place in Ghana and elsewhere on our continent. What it means is that Africa is ripe for a new revolution—an armed revolution.

10th April 1966

FELLOW countrymen, Chiefs and people, friends and comrades in the Convention People's Party, I want to take the opportunity on this Easter Sunday, 10th April 1966, to speak to you again from the Voice of the Revolution, Radio Guinea, Conakry. I sent you my warmest Easter Greetings and I wish you an enjoyable Easter holiday, if you are in a position to have one. I know it is hard for you to forget the trials and tribulations and humiliation which you have passed through within the last forty-six days, since the 24th of February, but it is high time for you now to wake up and survey the extent of the degradation, insults and abuses which some army and police officers have brought upon Ghana.

The sins and crimes of the so-called National Liberation Council are an affront to Ghanaian dignity and personality. These people have dragged Ghanaian manhood and womanhood into the street, lanes and gutters, but I know that by this time you have got over the shock and have composed yourselves enough to take stock of what has taken place around you.

This petty-minded clique of army and police rebels who have had the effrontery to claim that they have taken over the government of Ghana are trying to conceal the truth from you. By intrigue and deception they have got control of the radio, the television and the newspapers and they are trying to blind your eyes, with a barrage of lies, to the crimes they are committing and the shame they have brought on our beloved country.

Fellow countrymen, my heart is heavy as I witness the damage which this clique of neo-colonialist conspirators are doing to our country. At the bidding of their overseas neo-colonialist masters they are dismantling the work of fifteen years. They are telling you that Ghana is bankrupt. They are telling you that our country is in debt to the extent of some £240 million. What fools they are! How ignorant for them to think that you believe these stupid lies! Open your eyes and look around you. See for yourselves. See the splendid new Tema Harbour. See the mighty Volta Dam. See the fine roads which we have built under the leadership of the Convention People's Party and its Government. See the schools, the colleges and the universities, see the clinics, hospitals, health centres and the facilities which we have created. See the factories which are already springing up. These are no debts. They are investments in our future as an independent nation. These are the physical guarantees of the bright, new future which I have promised you and which I have been working for. Together, we can put our Ghana firmly and squarely on its own feet. Together, we can create the things we need for ourselves instead of going cap-in-hand for charity handouts from foreign powers whose only wish is to exploit us and make us vassals to their interests.

I know these are hard and trying days for you. I have never tried to conceal from you that real independence (that is to say economic independence) does not come without hard struggle and sacrifice. Unlike the cheats and deceivers, the liars and traitors who are now trying to lord it over you, I have never promised you an easy road. I have respected your good sense, your capacity for work, your pride in yourselves and your sense of national dignity.

I have told you that before we can make real progress and raise our living standards to the highest level that is possible, we must put first things first. If you wish to construct a house you must first lay the foundations. You cannot start building in the air. It is the same with a nation. If you wish to build an economically independent nation you must lay the foundations in roads and water supplies and electricity and a modern harbour. You must educate your people and train them for the new skills that are necessary to operate an industrialisation programme. This is what we have been doing in Ghana. This has been the Work and Happiness Programme of the Convention People's Party. This is how we have been laying the foundations upon which to build a country which can stand up in equality to any country in the world.

I have often warned you that in trying to find this real freedom for ourselves we would have enemies. I have warned you of the intrigues that are taking place against us. You know that several times assassins have tried to destroy my life because they wish to destroy the policies for which I stand. Now they have shown their hands for all to see.

Why do you think these traitors—these agents and lackeys of colonialism and of international intrigue to destroy the independence of Ghana—chose this moment to perform their dastardly act? I will tell you. Less than one month before they struck to destroy all our hard work we had inaugurated the first electricity from the Volta Dam. Only three days before this treachery we had signed a new agreement to irrigate the mighty Accra plains.

At last all our effort was about to bear fruit. With the inauguration of our electric power from the Volta Dam nothing could now prevent our rapid forward march into a new industrial era. With the launching of a great new irrigation scheme nothing could prevent an enormous increase in our food-growing capacity. During these next years Ghana was all set for a tremendous march forward. There were to be thousands of new well-paid jobs. There was to be a mighty increase in food production. Plenty for all. This was the moment for which we had worked and striven. And this was the time these evil men and their neo-colonialist masters chose to strike.

At last we were on the threshold of a great new victory. We had in 1957 won our political independence after eight years of struggle. Now in 1966 we were at the threshold of winning our economic independence.

The same people who tried to sabotage our winning of political independence nine years ago have now struck to sabotage our economic independence, and are systematically dismantling our socialist gains and achievements.

They have thrown away our Seven Year Plan on which we had worked so hard and in the formulation of which we had had been assisted by some of the best economic brains from all over the world. They are promising to dismantle the industries which we have sacrificed so much to set up.

What criminal foolishness! What inveterate madness! These lackeys and traitors, these quislings of colonialism will plunge our country into chaos and into a new servitude if they are not checked at once.

What are they offering to put in the place of our development plans? What are they offering in place of our socialist gains and achievements? Instead of having pride in their country and wishing it to stand on its own feet, instead of trusting you to have pride in yourselves and in your country, they are surrendering everything for which we have worked and are crawling like abject beggars to overseas moneylenders for miserable handouts to try to escape from the wreckage of their own folly and stupidity.

And what are they getting? From West Germany they have been promised £3½ million! Have they no pride? Have they no sense of decency towards their own people? What a miserable payment for the sale of the birthright of our struggle. It means that the villains who compose the self-styled National Liberation Council are nothing but ignorant men—men without economic and political foundations. Promises of food "aid" to Ghana? What an insult! Ghana is not a starving country. What Ghana needs are big long-term loans at very low rates of interest to build up and strengthen her industries, improve her factories and diversify her agriculture.

Yes, I have borrowed money on your behalf, but I have borrowed it upon the basis of building tangible assets, such as the Volta Dam. And I have made sure that the international agreements which I have signed have a basis of economic feasibility and that the money we borrow can create something lasting and beneficial not only to ourselves in our lifetime but for the generations which are to follow us. I have believed that it was our duty to create a Ghana of which our successors might be proud and for which they might remember us with gratitude and honour.

But these irresponsible upstarts are selling our birthright for the miserable handouts that can benefit no one. Men and women of Ghana, do you want to become beggars satisfied to receive occasional crusts of bread from the heavily-laden tables of foreign exploiters who are now flooding into Ghana like vultures picking the tastiest morsels from the carcase of our shame, leaving for our Ghanaian masses only the bare bones of their greed?

Fellow Ghanaians! This must not happen. We have pride in ourselves. We have pride in our Nation. Do not let it go down in history that we were the ones who permitted the betrayal of the heritage that it is our duty to leave to our children.

Rise up and destroy this clique of arrogant traitors and servile lackeys of neo-colonialism. Their ugly heads should not be allowed to appear any more in Ghana.

Fellow Ghanaians, these are harsh days for all of us. They are days when we must be staunch and fight to destroy this so-called National Liberation Council, if we are not to sink into abject servitude. Our country is being destroyed and brought to shame in the eyes of the world by this shameless clique of traitors.

Some of you may not know *all* that is now happening in Ghana, nor *all* that is going on in Accra. Strict censorship and control of the means of information is being used to suppress the truth. But people coming out of Ghana are telling terrible stories of repression and murder, sadism and rape that are shaming our country in the eyes of the civilised world.

Before the traitorous and the rebellious "National Liberation Council" tried to usurp power during my absence from Ghana, Ghana was a haven to which the oppressed from all parts of Africa could come to carry on their struggle. It was a haven for freedom fighters for independence and against colonialism. The name of Ghana was revered all over the African continent as a staunch friend of the oppressed. African brothers from South Africa, from Rhodesia, from Mozambique and Angola, from so-called Portuguese Guinea and the Cape Verde Islands and other oppressed colonial areas were given hospitality amongst us. Do you think that this is something of which we needed to be ashamed? Not at all; on the contrary, it was something of which we should be justly proud. Haven't we proclaimed that the independence of Ghana is meaningless unless it is linked up with the total liberation of Africa?

Now hundreds of these brave freedom fighters who came to our country trusting us to look after them and help them in their struggle against colonial oppression and believing as we do that Africa and the struggle for freedom is indivisible, these brave men and women have been sent back—bag and baggage by this traitorous clique—to the countries from which they had fled to seek refuge, inspiration and protection in Ghana. Comrades, what can we do to undo the shame which this evil "National Liberation Council" has brought upon Ghana? The so-called National Liberation Council must be crushed and destroyed at once otherwise the dignity of Ghana and the glory of Africa will be compromised. Countrymen, my heart bleeds and I know you shed tears of shame when we were told of brother Africans who have been sent from the soil of Ghana back into the hands of assassins who, I understand, have now put many of them to death.

Fellow Ghanaians, I ask you if you are standing, to sit now by your radio sets as I am now sitting before the microphone through which I speak to you, and I ask you to raise your hand in our Convention People's Party salute and swear to act from now.

Countrymen, these are the terrible facts which are now coming out of Ghana and being told to the world. The whole world knows that Ghana is now being subjected to a rule of guns and bayonets directed by a clique of shamelessly ignorant men who by deception have beguiled some of my army and police officers and men. The whole world is beginning to realise that under these ignorant renegades—this so-called "National Liberation Council"—the fabric of law and order is breaking down.

Let me tell you what Mr. Geoffrey Bing, Q.C., and former British Member of Parliament told the British press after he had been released from prison where he was unlawfully incarcerated by the self-styled National Liberation Council. You know that Mr. Bing was one of my legal advisers. He is a distinguished lawyer who had come to Ghana at our invitation to help us in our legal and constitutional work. This is how the rebel soldiers treated him on the instigation and direction of the so-called National Liberation Council.

The soldiers, he said, tore all his clothes from his body except for his underpants. Then, refusing to allow him to untie the laces, they tore the shoes from his feet, causing him injury and pain. Then they forced him to march barefoot across a rough courtyard so that the stones cut his feet. They stuck a bayonet into him and his back became smothered with blood. Then they made him sit in a corner and, as he says: "I thought I was going to be shot." The soldiers of the "National Liberation Council" tortured him by making him stand up and sit down in repeated succession without being able to use his hands. Only when the Commander of the Ghana Navy came upon the scene did they stop torturing him.

24

You know that Mr. Bing is no criminal. He was our guest, helping in our national work. Yet this is how he has been treated by this sadistic "National Liberation Council." Nor is this all. While Mr. Bing was kept in gaol at the mercy of these sadistic soldiers of the "National Liberation Council" his wife was attacked and molested by other soldiers of the "National Liberation Council." If the "National Liberation Council" can do this to Mr. and Mrs. Bing then they must have done worse to my Ministers and the Members of Parliament whom the "National Liberation Council" now holds in prison. Imagine what the women amongst them must have gone through: brutality, sadism, molestation and rape.

Fellow Ghanaians, friends and comrades, these evil things are not of your doing, but it is the duty of us all to restore the good name of Ghana so that once more it may be heard with respect throughout the world.

I shall be speaking to you again, but today, Easter Sunday, I make this appeal to you. Do not surrender your minds to the barrage of lies which is being hurled out. Do not surrender your morals and your self-respect to the infamies which are being carried out in the name of Ghana by the "National Liberation Council." Do not surrender your dignity to traitors and self-seekers. Stand up proudly as true Ghanaian men and women. Remember your heritage. Remember the struggles we have carried out together. Take pride in your history. Have faith in the future.

Fellow countrymen, friends and comrades, the hour of deliverance is approaching. And as I said in my last broadcast, it will not be long and I shall be with you again. All you must do now is to prepare yourselves. Organise yourselves into an irresistible force in the regions, villages, towns and cities. Let each one of you become the centre of organisation to overthrow the traitors and the renegades who call themselves the "National Liberation Council." My coming to Accra will be obvious to you. When you see the signs of my coming you must come out en masse and join hands with those who will be revolting against this shameless and wicked clique of rebels. The evil set-up—the so-called National Liberation Council —should be crushed and destroyed, never to be allowed to raise its dirty head again on the soil of Ghana. I know that when the time comes some of them will try to run away from

Ghana. Don't let them. I charge you all with the responsibility for keeping vigilant eyes on them; for their days of reckoning are fast approaching.

I know that the greater majority of the army is still loyal to me and that those that have been dragged into this sordid and treacherous affair by the self-styled National Liberation Council are, or 'were, misled by clever deception. To them I say, 'it is time to wake up, stand firm and break through the flimsy bands of deception with which the so-called National Liberation Council holds you. Do not co-operate with this ignorant and shameful clique. Rather, prepare: come out boldly and strike down the renegades. Save the prestige and good name of Ghana—that prestige which we have so nobly built up by self-sacrifice and hard work.'

I call upon the Trades Union Congress of the country to play their part by organising strikes and boycotts, if necessary, sabotage. I still remember the part played by the Railway Workers' Union during the pre-independence days. The same men who made independence possible are there now in Ghana; I call upon them to act now. Let us act and destroy these evil men and re-build quickly what they have destroyed. The shame and disgrace they have brought upon Ghana must be wiped out as quickly as possible. You must rise again and save the nation from this group of cheats and idiots before they heap too much disgrace upon Ghana and cause too much damage to our country.

Look at the country now and see what they have already done to Ghana. Is this the Ghana we know? Is this the Ghana we have built up by dint of hard work and self-denial? Already, black marketeering runs wild in the country, prices of foodstuffs soar high as food shortages grow rampant. The cost of living rises uncontrollably. Building and constructional projects undertaken by my Government have all come to a standstill.

I hear that the borders of Ghana are being opened to every Tom, Dick and Harry to enter and leave the country as he pleases. If this is done, how are the nation's life and economy to be protected? And this is precisely what these political idiots have done.

Countrymen, by the folly of their actions, this stupid clique of renegades have disturbed the balance of forces holding

Ghana together and they are too ignorant and stupid even to understand that. They have thrown Ghana into confusion and chaos. They have condemned the country to an even more confused and chaotic future and the pity of it is that they have not the economic foundations nor the political acumen to forestall this. The rebels have also abolished the constitution of chieftaincy. The people of Ghana are not going to lie down unconcerned for their achievements and traditions to be trampled down by this notorious clique of ignorant army and police adventurers.

Today, night has fallen and darkness prevails in Ghana. But tomorrow it will be noon and light will appear again in Ghana as naturally as day follows the night.

Another point which I want to make clear about my coming is that I am not depending on any foreign power to help me to invade Ghana, so no country should be unjustly and childishly accused or blamed for organising any army to come and fight Ghana. The Ghanaian masses themselves will rise to overthrow this clique of army rebels. The people of Ghana are their own liberators. We fought and won against colonialism and imperialism. How much less is the task of vanquishing a handful of internal rascals and dupes.

I do not want to mention the names of those who constitute the self-styled "National Liberation Council." They are not fit to be mentioned. They are not even worth the chairs they sit on at the Police Headquarters. Incidentally, why not use army chairs? Why police chairs? Look at the very composition of the "National Liberation Council" and heaven save Ghana from the hands of this clique of army and police adventurers and gangsters. We will not tolerate them for long. They and everything they stand for must be crushed and destroyed now. There is victory for us!

Countrymen: Africa is not dismayed by the events which have taken place in Ghana and elsewhere in our continent. What it means is that Africa is ripe for a new revolution—an armed revolution. A new phase of the African revolution has been reached. This revolution must overcome and triumph over imperialism, racialism and neo-colonialism. It must finally usher in the total emancipation and the political unification of our continent. Africa must be free; Africa must be united.

Countrymen, I shall be speaking to you again from Radio

Guinea's "Voice of the Revolution" on 61.10 metre band, 4910 kilo cycles and 31.08 metre band, 9650 kilo cycles. Be sure to tune in. Tell your friends and comrades. Let them join you to hear my messages to you. You will hear me personally in English on Sundays from 8 p.m. to 11 p.m., and my messages will be relayed to you in the local Ghanaian languages on Mondays, Wednesdays and Fridays at 7 p.m.

Next time I will tell you some of the things you must now do to vanquish the traitors. There is victory for us!

Forward ever, Backward never
Long live the people of Ghana
Long live the Convention People's Party
Long live the African revolutionary struggle
Long live a totally free and united Africa

6. Your united strength is invincible. Only organise. Organisation decides everything. Organise in the villages, in the towns and in the cities—in the lanes and gutters where the "N.L.C." has dragged you.

24th April 1966

FELLOW Ghanaians, men and women, friends and comrades, today is the 24th of April, exactly two months since the "Notorious Liars Council" which deceptively styles itself "National Liberation Council," traitorously undermined the state and government of Ghana and attempted to assume political power. This clique of traitors, by their act, have brought untold shame and disgrace upon Ghana—Ghana which was in the forefront of the African Revolutionary Movement, Ghana which was the centre of gravity of the African struggle; Ghana which was the vanguard of African Unity and Socialism; Ghana which was the home of African Freedom Fighters, a political asylum and a refuge for those who sought to escape the intrigues of imperialism, colonialism and racialism. Countrymen, before our very eyes, this Ghana we built by selfless hard work is being reduced by this notorious clique of neo-colonialist adventurers to a politically insignificant and third-rate state.

The brains and loyal cadres of the Civil and Public Services and competent members of the Army and Police who are loyal to me and the Nation, have either been killed, imprisoned or temporarily subdued by torture and intimidation. I call upon Ghanaians everywhere to act quickly and save their land and country from this clique of neo-colonialist stooges and lackeys. Law and order are fast breaking down in Ghana. Go through the streets of Accra today and, alas, you only see widespread burglary, stealing, extortion, intimidation and brigandage; bullying, insulting and molesting men, women and children. Everywhere now, there is lawlessness, a lawlessness that walks hand in hand with those who were supposed to uphold the law. This is the sad and shameful state to which the so-called National Liberation Council has dragged our proud country within the last two months. Of course, the neo-colonialist and imperialist press is conveniently blind to all these atrocities being perpetrated inside Ghana now. Their press in silent over this; they only hear the lies.

Just take a look at this "Notorious Liars Council" and you will find that they are made up of only corrupt and neo-colonialist puppets. Indeed, their corrupt nature is one of the root causes for their treachery.

Not long ago, I had investigations made into the rampant wave of diamond racketeering. It was revealed that certain high-ranking officers in the Police Service were directly implicated in this diamond racketeering. But current world problems forced me to desist from immediate drastic action apart from throwing their expatriate collaborators out of the country. In order to cover and protect themselves from public shame they instigated this rebellion when I was away on the invitation of President Ho Chi Minh to visit Hanoi. They cleverly got certain army officers of weak moral character like Ankrah, Kotoka and Afrifa roped into the deal. Then acting under the advice and instruction of their neo-colonialist masters deceptively lied to some of my soldiers that I was going to send them to Vietnam to fight a war that is not their cause. It was due to the fear of these police officers that their diamond racketeering connections might be revealed that Mr. G. Bing was not brought to court or even to any of their stage-directed press conferences.

Since the 24th February rebellion, these corrupt traitors have brought back their collaborators in diamond racketeering in order to continue their nefarious traffic. But I assure them that sooner than their masters expect we shall throw them out again on their ears.

Fellow Ghanaians, now that the shock is over and stupe-faction has died out, I call upon the officers and men of the armed forces who are loyal to me, their President and Supreme Commander with the support of the Party and the people to come out boldly, without fear, and wipe off this blot on Ghana by destroying the existence of this so-called National Liberation Council.

I call upon you to act quickly before the respect and the reputation which the Ghana Army and Police have had is totally destroyed and replaced by a horrible image of rene-gades and lackeys. I call upon you to act and save Ghana from further humiliation and disgrace. I call upon the rank and file of the Convention People's Party, the Houses of Chiefs in all the nine regions of Ghana, the Trade Unions of the country, the Farmers' Councils, the Ghana Moslem Council, all Women's Organisations (including Market Women), the Ghana Young Pioneers, Workers' Brigade and Railway and Harbour workers: All of you should come out together to overthrow this selfish clique of adventurers and save Ghana from further national disgrace.

The traitors are not only dismantling our industrial and agricultural projects. They have also attacked our educational system. The standard of secondary schools and universities is being reduced. The free educational system which, with hard work, I and my government embarked upon is being disrupted and set back.. The University College of Cape Coast which would soon have been declared a University is being downgraded to the level of a Teacher Training College. My plan for the establishment of a University College of Agriculture has been set aside by this notorious clique of lying adventurers. Several government scholarships awarded to students at home and abroad have been cancelled or withdrawn and thousands of our Ghanaian students still studying abroad have been ordered to abandon their studies and go back home.

To these unfortunate students I say: do not be discouraged. Go back home and suffer your frustration with quiet fortitude. Bide your time and rise with the masses to trample down these irresponsible and ignorant anarchists. It will not be long and I shall be with you again and you will take up once more the threads of your academic pursuits which have been so treacherously severed by the so-called National Liberation Council. At home in Ghana, the traitorous rebels have even sunk so low as to cut the legitimate National Lottery winnings accruing to individuals.

Indeed, this ignorant clique in army and police uniforms have abandoned most of the profitable projects undertaken by my government and set aside my government's carefully planned development programme. These traitors say the country's economy is breaking down and there is no money to finance this or maintain that national project. But barely two months ago the Convention People's Party and my government were doing all these efficiently and it was our principle never to crawl to any foreign power begging for measly handouts. Today, this principle is being shamelessly trodden down to our humiliation. The so-called National Liberation Council is an opprobrium to Ghana. The traitors say the country's economy is collapsing, but only two months ago we were solidly on our own feet and progressively implementing our Seven-Year Development Plan.

Countrymen, this ignorant clique of neo-colonialist lackeys are so economically dense and politically backward that they are incapable of planning the financing of even a small industrial project. It is no surprise if the intricate problems of National Economy prove too much a task for their limited mentalities.

The traitors are totally unprincipled and wholly unaware that even ruling by decrees must have a principle. Daily, their unprincipled, ignorant and irresponsible actions plunge Ghana into deeper chaos and confusion. This is why the people of Ghana must rise en masse and save themselves from these traitors. Otherwise their suffering will have no end. The independence we fought for so hard will be lost. You will become another neo-colonialist country, you will return to your colonial past, economically dependent on foreign neo-colonialist powers and blindly taking orders from foreign neo-colonialist masters.

Over the last two months, Ghana has been under a highly irresponsible set-up of neo-colonialist agents and stooges. This must come to an end. People of Ghana, this is your hour, this is your time. Arise and overthrow this clique of ignorant neo-colonialist adventurers. This is the moment to end the hardship and suffering which have been brought upon you by this so-called National Liberation Council.

Already, the total loss of revenue within two months of the so-called National Liberation Council's misrule by decrees is estimated in terms of millions. Our revenue is running down steeply without yielding anything profitable to the state of Ghana due largely to the administrative incompetency and political and economic mismanagement of this Notorious Liars Council.

Today, racketeers, smugglers, profiteers, spivs and swindlers are those the "National Liberation Council" are allowing to enter Ghana. Yesterday, the men and women who were building Ghana into a place where men and women can live irrespective of race, colour or religion have all been thrown out or imprisoned as if they were criminals.

Fellow Ghanaians, men and women, how long is this state of affairs going to be tolerated in Ghana? There is only one answer. Arise and overthrow these stooges and puppets of neo-colonialism at once before they get rooted into our peaceful society. Your failure to do this will simply increase your misery. Do not wait for someone to come and tell you to act. Organise yourselves into action wherever you are and in whatever capacity and bring an immediate stop to this shameless clique. Organise yourselves and let each one of you be a centre of organisation with one aim; to crush this foreign inspired rebellion without delay. Delay means further humiliation and suppression. Their destruction is a job that must be done and done in quick time.

See the thousand and one Commissions of Inquiry into corporations and institutions. These corporations, unlike the so-called National Liberation Council, were set up legally and constitutionally for purposes of agricultural and industrial development. But why does the so-called National Liberation Council not set up an inquiry into the widespread diamond racketeering? Because, they know this will bring top swindlers of the Police Service, into the dock. This will show the masses why the so-called National Liberation Council is acting in the way it is.

Thousands of innocent people have been forcibly arrested at the point of bayonets and thrown into prison without the due process of law; yet this master-minded Council deceptively forced the announcement on Radio Ghana of the abolition of the Preventive Detention Act.

Those arrested and detained include respectable citizens, influential chiefs, all Members of Parliament, former Diplomats, Civil Service Officials, Public Officers, all District and Regional Commissioners, Local Councillors, Members of the Security Forces, Workers' Brigade Officers, Border Security Guards, loyal officers and men of the Army and Police, members of the Bar Association, Lecturers and Professors of Universities and many leading citizens whose names are before me but are too numerous to be mentioned individually. What crimes have they committed? The only crime of these thousands of people arbitrarily arrested and gaoled is their membership of the Convention People's Party and their unflinching loyalty to the socialist ideals of the Convention People's Party and its government. The so-called National Liberation Council think that by this wanton dictatorial action they can strangle the dynamic Convention People's Party, the vanguard of our socialist revolution. But, they might as well arrest the whole population of Ghana and declare the whole country one big prison cell! But this they cannot do. What are these stupid clique of renegades and neo-colonialist stooges after? How much did they get from their neo-colonialist bosses as payment for their treachery and for perpetrating such heinous crimes against the people of Ghana?

Never, since my government was given the people's mandate to govern, have we dared to govern the country by arbitrary decrees. What are the Bar Association and the Judiciary doing? Have they succumbed to the lawless idiocy and criminal lunacy of this notorious liars council that impudently calls itself a "National Liberation Council?"

Radio and television have become the propagatory media for lies and false propaganda. Even the voice of speakers shiver because they speak under force and duress. Under threats backed by guns and bayonets, they are forced to propagate lies reluctantly.

To the "National Liberation Council" perjury and raping are not criminal, and brigandage and theft are badges of honour. Of course, these offences never come on the Ghana radio but the news is notoriously widespread and flourishes far and wide around the globe.

Countrymen, ten years of heroic struggle and nine years of independence and consolidation, in other words, after nineteen years of heroic struggle to end colonialism and imperialism, this shameless clique of renegades and adventurers in conspiracy with neo-colonialism seek to put us back where we were in 1947! We cannot allow this to happen. We shall not allow them to succeed. We owe it to posterity, to our children and their children after them to save our socialist gains from these vandals and renegades. Indeed, we owe it to the African Revolution to save Ghana from the clutches of these stooges and lackeys of neo-colonialism.

Fellow Ghanaians, it is obvious that what the "National Liberation Council" is doing in Ghana is neither Ghanaian nor African. There are definitely the hands of foreign powers directing it. Its members echo their neo-colonialist masters' voice.

As I have continuously told you, the task of freeing Ghana from these traitors rests squarely with you Ghanaians. Only quick concerted action can save the situation and we must rise gallantly to take the task in hand. I have my plans. I am not resting and I know that we shall soon throw these rebels and their neo-colonialist masters out of Ghana. But eventual success depends on you, the masses of Ghana. The time has come to rise together and organise to resist these rebellious traitors. Have confidence in your united strength and rise to overthrow these renegades. As I told you in my former broadcasts, your united strength is invincible. Only organise. Organisation decides everything. Organise in the villages, in the towns and in the cities; in the lanes and gutters where the "National Liberation Council" has dragged you. Do not collaborate with these rebels and mutineers and soon they will be consumed in the heat of your anger. Organise sabotage and boycotts where you can do so safely. If guns, bayonets and bullets will not allow you to hold your Party meetings openly, hold them in secret, exchange ideas and mutual encouragement and plan and co-ordinate your organised resistance.

Countrymen, I assure you, I myself am not resting. Victory is imminent and I will be with you soon.

Forward ever, Backward never. There is victory for the Ghanaian Socialist Revolution and the African Revolutionary Socialist Struggle.

> Long live the people of Ghana
> Long live the African Revolutionary Struggle
> Long live the Continental Union Government of Africa
> Long live the Militant States of Organisation of African Unity (the O.A.U.)
> Long live the African Freedom Fighters
> Long live the African Liberation Movement

7. The so-called National Liberation Council is selling the country to neo-colonialism. . . . . Unless these stooges are destroyed quickly, Ghana will soon return to its colonial past.

1st May 1966

FELLOW Ghanaians, friends and comrades of the Convention People's Party, workers and farmers of Ghana, once again I speak to you from Conakry on Radio Guinea's "Voice of the Revolution." These messages from me which will come to you from time to time are meant to fortify and encourage you in these times of trial, morale-weakening and humiliation, false and vicious lies and propaganda fiendishly calculated to deceive you and undermine your faith in our Ghanaian Revolution.

Countrymen, today is May Day, the 1st of May. It is set aside as a symbolic commemoration to international workers solidarity. On this May Day my "message" is particularly directed to the workers, peasants and farmers of Ghana.

Comrades, on this day the workers and peasantry throughout the world re-assert their socialist consciousness and their political awareness. I know that this year guns and bayonets of a traitorous clique will not allow you to celebrate this great day, but I promise you, we shall celebrate it doubly next year.

In our Ghanaian revolutionary struggle which culminated into independence on the 6th of March 1957, the workers of Ghana rose with us and together we launched "Positive Action," now famous in our history. In the success of our struggle for independence, considerable credit must go to the workers and farmers of Ghana.

In our national reconstruction and socialist development you have been indispensable. You have organised yourselves into effective trade unions and co-operatives throughout the country.

Workers of Ghana, this is not the occasion for me to remind you of your sacrifices and successes.

This year finds the workers and farmers of Ghana facing times which test your very existence and that of the nation you have helped to build. Our Ghana Trades Union Congress, a spearhead in our revolutionary struggle, is now in jeopardy.

Since independence, imperialists and neo-colonialists with their lackeys and stooges have spared no effort or money in many a vicious vendetta to undermine and sabotage our economic advance. By intrigues and subversion they sought through their puppets to re-establish another hold on Ghana. But our workers and farmers, under the dynamic leadership of the Convention People's Party kept them at bay.

Now, when my attention was turned to the international problem of world peace, our imperialist and neo-colonialist enemies have temporarily succeeded in instigating and engineering a neo-colonialist army-police rebellion in Ghana. In order to commit this outrage against Ghana they resorted to the bribery and corruption of certain army and police officers whom they bought to do their dirty job for them. These traitorous puppets and lackeys of imperialism and neo-colonialism are trying to sell Ghana for a mess of pottage. Certain foreign powers are daily directing them to do the things from which the neo-colonialist gains and Ghana loses. But these lackeys are too stupid and ignorant to see into their knavery and chicanery.

Workers and farmers of Ghana don't allow yourselves to be fooled and deceived by this neo-colonialist clique in Ghana. They are doing what their neo-colonialist masters tell them. They are in their pockets. After only two months of their misdeeds and misgovernment see what has come upon Ghana; prices of foodstuffs soaring high, shortages of food, black-marketing, smuggling. Where are the milk and the food which their neo-colonialist bosses promised them? Is there enough to go round? Another month and hunger and famine will engulf Ghana. Workers of Ghana, are you going to sit down and let disaster and misfortune overtake you through the actions of this clique of political idiots? Organise boycotts, strikes and sabotage! See that these neo-colonialist puppets are thrown out of Ghana.

The anti-people, anti-workers, anti-farmers and anti-socialist neo-colonialist attempt to subdue and exploit the workers and farmers through this clique of army and police traitors is now clear to you. Very soon, if you don't act now, they will "attack" and disband the trade unions as they have done already with other progressive peoples' organisations. Mark my word! I know how imperialism and neo-colonialism work through their puppets. If you don't act now they will turn Ghana into a fascist state and where will the workers be? They will even bury the Trades Union Congress. The reactionary and neo-colonialist counter-revolutionary agents and lackeys are openly and systematically destroying the gains and achievements of the workers and farmers of Ghana in the interests of their imperialist and neo-colonialist masters. Workers and farmers of Ghana, look at your agricultural and industrial achievements and ask yourselves: are we going to allow this clique of ignorant traitors and vandals to destroy our socialist gains and achievements in the interest of neo-colonialism? This is exactly what the so-called national liberation committee or council is going to do to you and Ghana. Act now by strikes and boycotts and sabotage and clean Ghana of their misdeeds and crimes. Workers of Ghana, this is not all. The traitors have also abandoned most of our development projects and state enterprises thus throwing thousands of workers out of employment. Most of our state-owned industries and factories have also been closed down; others are threatened. The so-called National Liberation Council is selling the country to neo-colonialism. What can be more anti-social than this? What can be more encouraging to capitalist exploitation? The traitors have abandoned our import and foreign exchange restrictions, and have thus opened Ghana's economy to the vagaries of foreign interests and domination. The Ghana currency is in difficulties. Foreign exchange has completely run down. Inflation is in the offing. By their irresponsible actions they have undermined Ghana's economic progress. Unless these stooges are destroyed quickly Ghana will soon return to its colonial past. Imagine, then, what will be your lot. The workers will no longer be working for themselves and their country and nation but for foreign interests.

Comrades, this is why the imperialists and neo-colonialists are happily congratulating the traitorous stooges and lackeys. They are doing so because they see bright opportunities for exploiting Ghana and the Ghanaians once again at the expense of the Ghanaian and Ghana.

Workers of Ghana, we cannot allow this to continue. Don't let it even happen. Comrades, what can be more gratifying than to be able to buy made-in-Ghana articles in our own country? Today the so-called National Liberation Council is acting so foolishly as to destroy all the state-owned factories.

Workers and farmers of Ghana, by this rebellion you have everything to lose and nothing to gain. The only people who stand to profit are the members of the "National Liberation Council." These traitors have staked claims for huge shares in the distribution of interests in Ghana. They have created for themselves ridiculously absurd positions with no other consideration but the salaries which go with them. Whoever heard of a Lieutenant--General in an "army" comprising only six battalions or the creation of an Inspector-General of Police in a small police service like ours? The term itself smells of colonialism. These stooges of neo-colonialism and imperialism are so much absorbed in their own selfishness and pomposity that they are even oblivious to ridicule. Their foolhardiness is almost surprising. Only a fool chooses to govern by martial law.

Comrades, today in Ghana, no loyal worker is safe from this clique of renegades. Innocent citizens have been murdered in cold-blood and thousands have been arbitrarily arrested and illegally thrown into prison. Innocent workers have been summarily dismissed and the progressive elements in our Ghanaian society are being suppressed, jailed or eliminated. Everywhere you see victimisation and intimidation backed by tommy-guns and bayonets. Today they may sack or victimise progressive workers at the Broadcasting and Television House, tomorrow they will "attack" another group of workers and yet another the next day, heartlessly leaving a trail of unemployed workers. Workers of Ghana, organise yourselves into a resistance-front and none will dare to oppose you. Your mass strength is invincible. The so-called National Liberation Council may hold guns and bayonets but it is the workers, the farmers and the people who in the final analysis decide. Without your support they can do nothing. Organise yourselves and resist and you will easily and quickly overthrow these lackeys of neo-colonialism. Do not be intimidated by the guns and bayonets. There are many in the army and police who are loyal to me and the Party and who are ready and waiting, at the right moment, to overthrow these stooges and puppets of neo-colonialism.

Workers of Ghana, are you going to sit down and watch all our hard-won achievements and gains being destroyed?

Are you going to sacrifice our socialist aspirations and betray Africa's confidence in you and Ghana? How long are you going to allow this shame and blot on Ghana to continue? I have confidence in your political awakening and on this May Day I call upon you to rise together and save Ghana from these capitalist and neo-colonialist agents of destruction. I call upon the progressive workers of the Trades Union Congress to rise and uproot all anti-socialist elements from our society. Do not condone the existence of this so-called National Liberation Council. Arise! Organise and strike against its existence. Do not be intimidated by guns, bayonets or threats of dismissal. These lackeys and stooges of imperialism and neo-colonialism have resorted to the extremes of political action and hope to disrupt the settled order of the working masses of our Ghanaian people; but they are bound to fail, in fact they have failed. They have indeed misfired. Soon we will rebuild and reinstate all that they have destroyed. We built them and we can build them again. There is victory for Ghana. There is victory for Africa.

Long live the Workers and Farmers of Ghana
Long live the Trades Union Congress of Ghana
Long live the All-African Trade Union Federation
Long live the Convention People's Party

8. Workers of Africa unite—unite and fight for socialism; unite and fight for a continental Union Government of Africa. . . . You have nothing to lose, but a new world to gain.

1st May 1966

May Day Message to the Workers of Africa

WORKERS of Africa, May Day, the 1st of May, is an international day on which the workers of the world close their ranks in international solidarity and dedicate themselves anew to the struggle for the working-class emancipation. In Africa it is a day for the workers of Africa to dedicate themselves anew in their fight against capitalist exploitation and foreign domination. In this struggle the workers of the world have one common aim: Socialism.

Workers of Africa, the battle against imperialism and neo-colonialism can never be won victoriously unless you organise yourselves on a Pan-African basis and fight with united effort. The unity of the workers of Africa is not only essential for the successful eradication and exclusion of all forms of capitalist exploitation from Africa but is also essential for African Unity and the struggle for a continental Union Government of Africa.

It was with this in view that the All-African Trades Union Federation (A.A.T.U.F.) was organised with its Headquarters in Accra with the central aim to unite and spearhead all the workers' movements in Africa. Only with this aim can the workers of Africa hold themselves against the forces and manoeuvres of reaction, imperialism and neo-colonialism and safeguard their socialist aims and aspirations. Unless the workers of Africa are united under *one* banner and developed as a bastion for action, the progress of political movement in Africa will always be militated against by imperialism and its kindred forces.

So workers of Africa come together and help in the eradication of neo-colonialism from Africa; come together and join hands with the revolutionaries and the freedom fighters engaged in the struggle not only to free and unite Africa but also to develop the basis for socialism. In fact every worker in Africa must be a revolutionary.

African Unity and a Continental Union Government of Africa are the pre-requisites for respect and dignity for Africa, so workers of Africa unite—unite and fight for socialism; unite and fight for a continental Union Government of Africa; unite and fight for the total and complete liquidation of imperialism and neo-colonialism in Africa.

You have nothing to lose but the fetters of oppression and suppression. You have nothing to lose, but a new world to gain.

Long live the workers of Africa
Long live Socialism
Long live African Unity
Long live the All-African Trade Union Federation

9. No amount of lies and false propaganda can alter the fact that by their deception, treachery, arrogance and corruption, the so-called National Liberation Council and their neo-colonialist supporters have earned the hatred and contempt not only of the Ghanaian people but also of all Africa. These renegades have betrayed the national character of Ghana and its African Personality.

8th May 1966

FELLOW Ghanaians, men and women, friends and comrades, once again I speak to you from Conakry on Radio Guinea's "Voice of the Revolution."

In the first place, I want you to know that the incident of 24th February 1966, that took place in Accra is not a coup d'etat but a counter-revolutionary rebellion. By this time its true nature and character should be clear to you all. Its nature is counter-revolutionary and its character pro-imperialist, neo-colonialist. The urgent questions you should be asking yourselves now are: Who are behind it? Who were the instigators of this rebellion? And who are supporting it? Who have made such utter fools of some of our army and police officers and men? The answers are obvious. Certain army and police officers lacking in character and ideology have become stooges and lackeys and have joined hands in conspiracy with the forces of neo-colonialism to destroy Ghana and reduce it to its colonial past. These renegades by staging the incident of 24th February 1966, thought they had found a clever escape from the just punishment for their diamond racketeering and smuggling activities.

The external character of this rebellion is clearly shown by the speed and alacrity with which certain Western powers recognised the rebellion and gave it their support. Western instigation and sponsorship of this rebellion is also shown from the way in which the Western press and news agencies became the propaganda agents of the so-called National

Liberation Council. It is an open secret in Ghana that the slogans and placards used in the staged demonstrations in Accra were printed in some of the Western embassies in Ghana. The way school children were dragged from their classrooms at the point of guns to go and demonstrate is wholly alien to the Ghanaian mind, character and tradition, and could only have been thought of by the twisted imperialist and neo-colonialist mentality. Indeed, behind all the activities of the so-called National Liberation Council stands the invisible "government" of neo-colonialism.

Countrymen, the fact that this rebellion was instigated from outside is obvious. The first attack was directed against the ideological centres of the Convention People's Party, for instance: the Party Headquarters, the Ideological Institute at Winneba, the offices of "Spark," the socialist mouthpiece of Ghana's socialist revolution, the Bureau of African Affairs and the African Affairs Centre. These were the centres not only of Ghanaian socialist revolution but of African revolutionary struggle. The editor of the "Spark," Mr. Kofi Batsa, was badly beaten up and at the moment we do not know his whereabouts; I hope he is alive, but he may be dead.

Why did they attack these centres? They attacked these centres because they know that the centres were the homes of our African freedom fighters and they thought by doing so they were attacking the source of Ghana's independence and that of the African revolution.

Take another example. The imperialist and neo-colonialist directed Notorious Liars Council say they have abolished Founder's Day? It is ridiculous. After all someone must have founded the new Ghana Nation and established it as a State. This is a matter of history and no neo-colonialist inspired stooge and traitor can alter it. And why abolish Republic Day? Ghana is a Republican State. In fact a socialist Republic! If Ghana is not a Republic then what is it? A dominion, a con-dominion or the colony of an invisible government? If the renegades say they have abolished Republic Day then why don't they follow the dictates of their imperialist masters and abolish the celebration of 6th March, our Independence Day, too? The 24th of February is not a liberation day but a day of national crime, sin, shame and anarchy. To celebrate it as a day of prayer is sacrilegious.

44

Countrymen, do not be discouraged by these stupid and senseless attempts to dismantle the symbols of our hopes, aspirations and achievements.

As you can see, the ghastly event in Ghana is not a mass revolt expressing mass discontent. It is not a national uprising against the government but it is carefully planned attack on the socialist trends and foundations of the Convention People's Party and the achievements of the workers and people of Ghana. It was conceived by a combination of neo-colonialists from outside and their counter-revolutionary lackeys in Ghana.

Countrymen, now that all our dreams and efforts to achieve a progressive and peaceful country are about to be realised these renegades who have always served the interests of imperialism and neo-colonialism now seek to set Ghana back, destroy its achievements and tear up the very constitution which has made these achievements possible. We shall not allow Ghana to become an economic colony of any foreign power or interest, neither shall we allow any neo-colonialist and imperialist inspired stooges and quislings to monkey about with the legal constitution of Ghana.

Through vicious lies and vile propaganda they have, by deception, forced a section of the army and police under their command to take sides with them in their sponsored neo-colonialist venture. Among other lies, the soldiers were led to think that the government was planning to disband the army of Ghana and replace it by a people's militia. The obvious nonsense inherent in this allegation is shown by the contradictory lie they told the soldiers about my government's intention to send the troops to fight in Vietnam and also in Southern Rhodesia. The neo-colonialist ravings about our realistic stand on the issue of our oppressed Zimbabwe brothers in Southern Rhodesia are mere psychological attempts to confuse the African nationalist awareness of the Ghanaian soldiers, and deceptively blind them to the truth and treachery of the so-called National Liberation Council.

As everyone in Ghana knows—soldier and civilian alike—not only did my government never intend to disband the Ghana Armed Forces but was actually doing all it could to reinforce them. A lot of nonsensical lies have also been told about the Presidential Guard Regiment in an attempt to deceive the soldiers into thinking that the Guard Regiment was something different from the main Ghana Army. The truth behind all these clumsy attempts to mislead, deceive and confuse our soldiers is that the great majority of the officers and men in the Ghana Armed Forces did not participate in this act of treachery and rebellion against the Ghana State, and in fact, most of the officers and men were strongly against it. This is why most of them have been disarmed and confined to barracks as if they were prisoners and criminals. But no amount of lies or false propaganda can alter the fact that by their deception, treachery, arrogance and corruption, the so-called National Liberation Council and their neo-colonialist supporters have earned the hatred and contempt not only of the Ghanaian people but also of all Africa. These renegades have betrayed the national character of Ghana and its African Personality.

Countrymen, the crime of these traitors and renegades is enormous. As you know, the modern history of our country falls into two principal stages. The first stage is the movement for independence which led to victory when, through Positive Action, the will of the people ended colonialism in Ghana. The next stage is the struggle for the consolidation of our independence and the setting up of a national economy free from the grip of foreign exploiters. This is the socialist way of development expressed in the Work and Happiness Programme of the Convention People's Party and embodied in our Seven-Year Development Plan. In these two stages of our struggle the enemy has always been one: foreign exploiters—imperialists and neo-colonialists.

During the first stage the struggle was difficult but the objective was quite simple: namely, to take over the positions occupied by the colonialists. The second stage is longer and much more difficult: the task is to keep the stronghold taken from the neo-colonialists and the colonialists, and to watch out that our enemy does not come back under new guises to colonise us again. The task is to organise, to build factories, to modernise and mechanise our agriculture, build roads, set up national co-operatives, national banks, state enterprises, and other progressive national institutions. In other words, the task is to raise our standard of living and give more work to the workers and farmers of the country. This calls for selfless dedication, self-denial and sacrifices from the masses and our Ghanaian people stood up to this challenge.

Our factories, our state farms, our roads, our universities, our schools and colleges, our hospitals, our Volta Dam, our Tema harbour and township, these are the concrete proofs of Ghana's forward march to prosperity and socialism. These socialist achievements of our country greatly reduced the field of activity of imperialist exploiters and that of their local agents and stooges. That is why they seek to destroy them. But who can take away from us the Volta Industrial Complex? Who can take away from the workers those state farms and factories? The people built them and the people will not allow a neo-colonialist set-up to hand them over to foreign and private interests. The workers will not stand for that sort of treachery. Machine-guns, rifles and bayonets cannot stand against the might of the masses of Ghana nor that of the workers of Ghana. We are moving forward and they know that we are on the correct road. Socialism means the liquidation of external and internal exploitation. If we are to build socialism, the interests of those that are exploiting us and their internal agents should be done away with.

It is not by mere coincidence that this rebellion happened almost immediately after our Minister of Finance, Mr. Kwesi Amoako-Atta, presented the new budget. The workers of Ghana knew that it was a worker's budget. Why has the so-called National Liberation Council set aside this year's budget as they have done our Seven-Year Development Plan? They know that this budget was not in the interest of their neo-colonialist masters. In the terms of this budget, taxes were levied on those earning more than £1,600 per annum, on the rents collected by landlords; and taxes were also put on the profits of all traders and merchants, especially those who were profiting from hoarding, black-marketing and conditional sales. The workers and people of Ghana know in whose interest this budget was prepared and whose interest it was to benefit.

Let our bereaved mothers and widows now in mourning know that even though for a time machine-guns and bayonets have become the law-makers of Ghana those who are respon-sible will face a ghastly retribution as sure as night follows the day; 2,500 murdered; more than 3,000 wounded, tortured and maimed; the savage rapes perpetrated against the women of Ghana; these are sins and crimes which cry to heaven for juśt retribution. Do these murderous renegades imagine that they will never have to give account to the people of Ghana for these crimes; murder, brigandage, rape and the bullet-torn corpses they bury at night on the Accra beaches? The bribes of neo-colonialists have cost a lot in terms of Ghanaian blood, dignity and self-respect. The Ghana Department of Statistics estimates that 25,000 workers are already thrown in the streets without work. It is further estimated that 350,000 Ghanaian workers will be out of jobs within the next few months. Can American powdered milk replace work for these workers?

Countrymen, they have devilishly deceived and misled a section of our armed forces and police in order to kill and murder their own brothers and sisters and to perpetrate untold hideous crimes against their own fathers and mothers; against their own friends and children; against their own country! These stooges stand exposed and condemned in the eyes of the people. They know that their end and destruction is near and that their neo-colonialist masters cannot even save them from the wrath of the Ghanaian people.

What has happened in Ghana is not a revolution. A true revolution is made by the masses, by the whole people in action; but this rebellion is only a mad attempt by frustrated neo-colonialism to re-colonise Ghana. The crime of these renegades is that they willingly accepted to do the dirty work on behalf of imperialism and neo-colonialism. In doing so they have committed high treason against the Ghana state. They are condemned for their crimes. The people of Ghana will execute the sentence. These neo-colonialist puppets forget that imperialists have no permanent friends. Their only permanent friends are their own interests.

People of Ghana arise to execute that sentence. There is victory for us. Forward ever, Backward never. People of Ghana arise and organise. People of Ghana arise and eradicate the enemy. Arise and destroy the so-called National Liberation Council. Arise and save Ghana from the hands of renegades and lackeys of neo-colonialism.

> Long the the African Revolutionary Struggle
> Long live the Freedom Fighters of Africa
> Long live the African Struggle for Socialism

10. There is no imperialist plot nor neo-colonialist intrigue that can halt the tide of the African revolutionary and liberation movement for the total economic emancipation of Africa and eventual political unification.

15th May 1966

FELLOW countrymen, men and women of Ghana, once again I speak to you from Conakry on Radio Guinea's "Voice of the Revolution."

A week ago today, I told you that the traitorous army-police rebellion in Ghana was instigated and sponsored by neo-colonialist enemies of Ghana and Africa. These enemies know the unflinching stand of Ghana against imperialism and neo-colonialism.

Ghana has always been feared and hated by the imperialists and the neo-colonialists. Immediately after independence I declared that Ghana's independence was meaningless unless it was linked up with the total liberation of Africa. Today, no less than 36 African states have also won their political independence. I have also pointed out that political independence could hardly be maintained without economic freedom and independence. The imperialists, colonialists and neo-colonialists, the racialists and settler regimes in Africa know this. That is why they ruthlessly seek to continue their exploiting control of the economy and natural resources of the "emerging" African states. In Ghana, our several state-owned factories and industries, state and co-operative farms and enterprises and our gigantic Volta River Complex have placed us in a position to industrialise and revolutionise our agriculture. This is the sure way we set about to achieve our economic independence. That is why—to the imperialists and the neo-colonialists—Ghana had become too dangerous an example to the rest of Africa to be allowed to continue under a socialist leadership.

Since our independence, our enemies have spared no effort or money in persistently and continuously undermining and sabotaging our progress and development. They have planned by bribery and corruption and intrigues to capture and destroy Ghana's economy. They have consistently tried to find the stooges and lackeys to do their dirty job for them. In this they have found their perfect tool in the so-called National Liberation Council. No less than six attempts have been made on my life through their puppets and quislings. In this vendetta against Ghana, the imperialists and their bought agents did not stop at anything even murder and assassination. By inhuman bombings, many Party members and activists, innocent men, women and children were wounded and maimed and some killed at Party rallies and meetings. In the 24th February recent neo-colonialist instigated rebellion, thousands of innocent Ghanaians have mercilessly been murdered. As late as only a week ago, bodies of people murdered in the streets and lanes of Accra still lay at the Korle Bu mortuary. Up to today, the clique of traitors, the so-called National Liberation Council has still not come out with the names of the unfortunate seven shamelessly buried with late Major-General Barwah of sad memory. But as I told you in my last broadcast, to the imperialists and neo-colonialists, the loss of Ghanaian lives means nothing, so long as they control the economy of the country. To them and their puppets who constitute the so-called National Liberation Council, treason, assassination, murder, pillage and the mass massacre and arrest of innocent citizens are no crimes at all. In fact, they are insensible to these crimes. That is why the traitorous Harley-Kotoka-Ankrah neo-colonialist clique of irresponsible lackeys directed by their imperialist and neo-colonialist masters and bosses, are doing everything to destroy the image of Ghana, her reputation, her prestige and honour.

Countrymen, the sole purpose of the imperialists and the neo-colonialists making use of certain sell-out and bought army-police officers in Ghana is to destroy our socialist gains and achievements. It is significant to note that in doing this they chose the politically ignorant, totally corrupt and nationally negative elements in the army and police. You can see from their actions that the notorious "National Liberation Council" are making no effort whatever to build but rather to destroy. People of Ghana, pause, look around you and reflect, and you immediately come to the sudden realisation and a rude awakening that the Ghana you so love is now turned upside down. Ruin, chaos, unemployment, hunger, poverty are beginning to engulf her. While the country's future is plunged deeper and deeper into the depths of economic and financial ruin and stagnation by their irresponsible and stupid actions, the ignorant so-called National Liberation Council is busily engaged in an ideological witch-hunt directed against the progressive elements in our society. They are so blind that they cannot see the insult and harm they are inflicting upon Ghana. They are only interested in setting up a thousand-and-one staged commissions of enquiry to look into this and that national organisation and state enterprise. And, of course, the traitors constituting the so-called National Liberation Council are afraid to set up a commission of enquiry to investigate the diamond racketeering and smuggling because they themselves are involved and implicated. Why not set up a commission of enquiry to investigate the property holdings of the members of the so-called National Liberation Council in Accra and outside Accra? It would be interesting to set up a commission of enquiry to investigate the financial and property holdings, houses, etc., of those who are now sitting in judgment over others. An investigation into their public and moral lives would produce a shocking revelation. The masses know of these holdings and are aware of the bribery, corruption and intrigue which was used to acquire them. And the masses know also why the Harley clique instigated certain army officers and dragged them into this rebellion.

Countrymen, while these neo-colonialist lackeys and stooges set up commissions of enquiry into everything except their ill-gotten properties and those of their friends and supporters, their neo-colonialist and imperialist masters daily direct them into irresponsible actions against Ghana. Those actions are deliberately calculated to destroy our socialist gains and achievements and undermine and sabotage the solid basis of economic independence which we have laid. They even tried to destroy my image. But they know that everybody knows that my life is an open book.

Through the foolish and ignorant actions of the so-called National Liberation Council, the state sector of our economy is being dismantled. Herein lie their neo-colonialist tendencies. By their unprincipled actions, the country's economy is declining and unemployment is increasing every day. On the directions of their imperialist and neo-colonialist masters, they are opening our borders to any Tom, Dick and Harry. They forget that by doing so they allow neo-colonialism to invade Ghana and dominate it. I wonder who are the economic and financial advisers of this so-called National Liberation Council. Do they not know that by their actions they are leading Ghana headlong into economic slavery? What they are doing are obvious methods of destroying the economy of Ghana. By this strategy, the imperialists and the neo-colonialists only seek to bring Ghana's economy into the sphere of their economic domination and subsequent exploitation. The opening of Ghana's borders is the surest way of bringing the economy of Ghana into the neo-colonialist grip. Through the "National Liberation Council" the imperialists and neo-colonialists seek to establish a wider sphere of economic subjugation over Ghana.

Countrymen, this neo-colonialist and imperialist instigated rebellion in Ghana is nothing more than a move in an imperialist, neo-colonialist plot to perpetuate the exploitation of the African people. They seek to destroy and strangulate the freely developing economies of independent African states and so force them into imperialist and neo-colonialist subordination. But they will fail because there is a new Africa and a new African who is awakened to his responsibilities. Africa is already re-awakened and progressive Africa will not allow them to succeed. There is no imperialist plot nor neo-colonialist intrigue that can halt the tide of the African revolutionary and liberation movement for the total economic emancipation of Africa, and her eventual political unification.

In Ghana, as elsewhere, the strategy of the imperialists and the neo-colonialists is to subvert by bribing and corrupting certain disgruntled elements in the country. In doing this they seek out and look out for the morally weak and those of colonial and neo-colonial mentality. These elements who now constitute the so-called National Liberation Council in Ghana, are so politically backward and economically dense that they even fail to see the obvious chicanery and evil motives and plans of their imperialist and neo-colonialist masters. These stooges and renegades are so totally selfish and unpatriotic that the only horizon they see is the extent of their own individual interests and inordinate personal ambition. By their political tomfoolery they run at the beck and call of their imperialist and neo-colonialist masters, hopping from one imperialist and neo-colonialist country to another for "Stand-by Funds." They do not even see and realise that the imperial-ists and the neo-colonialists never give "free aid." What they give with one hand they take with the other. Imagine sending an economic mission to these countries asking for "Stand-by Funds." What does that mean, anyway? Is it a loan or what? It is nothing but a financial sell-out of Ghana. They are too ignorant and are such stooges that the interest of Ghana is not their concern. The so-called National Liberation Council must be held responsible for the present decline of Ghana's economy.

Nor is that all. At home in Ghana, several thousands have been brutally killed, and all those who manned our administra-tion have been arbitrarily imprisoned. Daily, defenceless loyal citizens are being intimidated and humiliated while others are bribed and corrupted to tell lies, and to spread false propa-ganda against the Convention People's Party, its leadership and government. Life in our once peaceful beautiful Ghana has been heartlessly thrown into disarray. Because of their hideous crimes Accra now looks like a dying town—a deserted village. Shopkeepers close their shops earlier in the evening than normal. Market women pack up their wares and rush home before dusk and soon the streets are empty. Indeed, there is a self-imposed curfew in Accra and other towns and cities now under the grip of the notorious "National Libera-tion Council." Such is the nature of the fascist neo-colonialist set-up now in Ghana. And this is what the Western imperialist press shamelessly call "democracy."

Fellow Ghanaians, the time has come to rise up and throw this fascist neo-colonialist inspired clique and their masters out of Ghana. Do not be deterred by the guns nor the bayonets with which their rebel soldiers daily threaten you. As I have already told you there is only one power which no tommy-guns and rifles or bayonets can overcome. That power is the enthusiasm and the determination of a whole people in action.

Fellow Ghanaians, the time has come to act and you must act now to save Ghana from the grasping clutches of the so-called National Liberation Council. Remember that your mass strength cannot be overcome by tommy-guns, rifles and bayonets of "the men" of the so-called National Liberation Council. Arise and organise! Let organisation be your watchword. Organise in the factories; organise in your homes; organise in your workshops and in your farms; organise in your schools, colleges and universities; organise wherever you may be. Organise now and arise in your mass strength and overthrow these traitors and renegades. Their only interest is to sell our country to neo-colonialism. Men and women of Ghana, workers and farmers of Ghana, organise, arise and save our dear country from disgrace, dishonour and doom.

As I told you in my last broadcast, it will not be long and I shall be with you once again, and we shall together build what the so-called National Liberation Council has destroyed. We did it and we can do it again. I am sure that when the time comes the traitors and renegades who have destroyed so much of what we have built through selfless sacrifice will answer to us and the masses for the hideous crimes they have committed against Ghana and her people: the thousands they murdered directly or indirectly, those poor unnamed citizens to whom they gave collective burial on the wet and sandy beaches of Accra, and those who are still lying unidentified and unclaimed in cold mortuaries! There are hundreds of names I could mention whose whereabouts nobody knows, except the so-called National Liberation Council. There are also others who through beating up with butts of rifles have had their faces and bodies disfigured—like the Minister of Finance, Mr. Amoako-Atta. And may I ask: Where are Kofi Batsa, Brigadier Hassan, Provençal who is the Chairman of the Accra-Tema City Council?

Countrymen, never before has so much blood been shed by so few for no reason at all! Be vigilant. Soon, just retribution will be meted out to the perpetrators of these wanton acts of heartless butchery. People of Ghana, organise, arise and overthrow these fascist neo-colonialist oppressors. Arise! The hour of victory, deliverance and justice is at hand. There is victory for us.

> Long live the people of Ghana
> Long live the Workers and Farmers of Ghana
> Long live the dynamic Convention People's Party
> Long live the Freedom Fighters of Africa
> Long live the African Liberation Movement
> Long live Africa, free, independent and politically **united**

54

11. I know that now, in silence, you continue to suffer and be humiliated but you will wake up soon, and woe to the traitors.

22nd May 1966

FELLOW countrymen, men and women of Ghana, once again I speak to you from Conakry on Radio Guinea's "Voice of the Revolution."

Many requests have been reaching me from Ghana and other countries asking me to repeat some of my broadcast messages to you. But before doing so I would like to comment briefly on some of the more recent actions of the so-called National Liberation Council.

Countrymen, since the 24th February incident this traitorous and rebellious clique of imperialist and neo-colonialist agents continue daily to demonstrate their utter stupidity and ignorance. They seem confused and are getting more stupid, more ignorant and more foolish every day. The depth of stupidity and ignorance into which these renegades and quislings have sunk is simply shocking.

Their complete lack of knowledge of international matters is clearly shown by their recent stupid and senseless action in requesting Interpol to arrest me. This is a demonstration of abject stupidity and ignorance. It is simply ridiculous! Being shockingly ignorant and irresponsible themselves, these traitors who go by the name of "National Liberation Council" think that Interpol does not know its duties and obligations. This clique of traitors don't even know that Interpol has nothing to do with political matters—national or international. In their ignorance, they foolishly imagine that they can use that international body for their insane political and morbid ambitions. But Interpol knows better and does not bother with insane suggestions. But this is not the time to fill in the many shocking gaps in their little knowledge. The pity of it is that their ridiculously stupid and ignorant actions are perpetrated in the name of our dear Ghana and are dragging her every day into disgrace, dishonour and humiliation. By their actions, this ignorant clique of imperialist and neo-colonialist stooges and lackeys are stripping Ghana of her pride, dignity, honour and reputation.

Countrymen, the damage which these irresponsible hirelings are daily perpetrating against Ghana is heinous. That is why you have to wake up from from stupefaction and arise and somehow crush them.

By lies, calumny and falsehood they very vainly seek to undermine your faith in the very noble cause which you yourselves have furbished for Ghana.

In their vain attempt to heap calumny upon my person, these traitorous stooges thought it worthwhile to set up commissions of enquiry, and who knows how much money has been spent by the Ghanaian taxpayer for these purposeless enquiries!

To show the absurdity of it all, I will tell you a story: You all know the late Nii Pappoe Oti who was a prominent citizen, a Ga man and a staunch member of the Convention People's Party—in fact one of its foundation members. At one time he asked me to buy him a car because at about 95 years of age he could not walk properly; he needed a car and if I did that for him he would know that he really need not suffer in his last years. It was Ankrah of the "National Liberation Council" who brought the message to me. I bought a car which I presented to Nii Pappoe Oti. The presentation was made by this same Ankrah and comrade Provençal whose whereabouts I don't know at the moment. Ankrah came back and thanked me for my gesture. Perhaps the so-called National Liberation Council should set up a commission of enquiry to find out why I bought the car for Nii Pappoe Oti and whether it was not a crime or a prestige offer?

Countrymen, our radio and television services have been reduced to no less than mere media for the propagation of wild lies and cheap propaganda.

In their vain and clumsy attempts to brainwash the Ghanaian masses and divert their attention from the enormity of their treasonable crimes, these traitorous renegades continue telling lies and falsehoods on the radio and set up one commission after another. But these commissions are no more than dishonest means through which the irresponsible "National Liberation Council" seek to achieve their wicked ends. I wonder what the Judges sitting on these commissions think about these commissions! Why was Dr. Morton not allowed to speak openly and publicly when he hinted that

Ankrah was involved in a certain deal?

Very soon the corrupt traitors of the "National Liberation Council" and their internal and external neo-colonialist masters and advisers will realise the wisdom in the saying that those who live in glass houses do not throw stones.

I know that you the people of Ghana have seen through the stupid attempts to deceive you. I know you; and I have confidence in you. I know that very soon you will find a quick way to deal with these stooges and traitors. There are nearly eight million of us in Ghana, and I have not known the Ghanaian who has not got his wits by him. I know that now, in silence, you continue to suffer and be humiliated but you will wake up soon and woe to the traitors. You are forced to sit and watch your dignity and self-respect being callously trampled down. How long can you put up with the vandalism, sadism, banditry, murder and brutality of this so-called National Liberation Council? I also know that very soon you will arise and not only overthrow but destroy the "National Liberation Council," its existence and all that it stands for. There is victory for us.

As I mentioned earlier on, repeated requests have been reaching me for re-broadcasts of some of my messages to you. I wish to take this opportunity to repeat my broadcast message to you on the 20th of March. Don't switch off now. In a moment I will be speaking to you again.

12. **When a people rise against oppression, brutality and betrayal, they must do so without fear. After all, the people's revolution against oppression and misrule is made and won by the contest against odds. Therefore, people of Ghana, awake!**

29th May 1966

COUNTRYMEN, men and women of Ghana, once again I speak to you from Conakry on Radio Guinea's "Voice of the Revolution."

In my last broadcast to you a week ago, I commented on how Dr. Morton was quickly silenced when he publicly hinted that the traitor Ankrah was involved in some corrupt 'deal'. Even though Dr. Morton was not allowed to speak publicly, the hint he made is not lost to the Ghanaian masses. More revelations about the corrupt nature of the Notorious Liberation Council will come to light.

I am sure that by now most of you are aware of *how* the corrupt Kotoka-Ankrah-Harley clique attempted to blackmail Miss Mary Amartey. Acting on behalf of this corrupt clique an irresponsible lawyer approached poor Mary Amartey with the criminal proposal that in exchange for £10,000 the so-called National Liberation Council would release Ayeh Kumi whom they hold in detention. What can be more base! What can be more corrupt! But to the criminals constituting the so-called National Liberation Council these acts of corruption are the order of the day. But, how many other such corrupt and criminal blackmails still remain unexposed? How many thousands of pounds do the renegades of the "National Liberation Council" and their agents amass as ransom for the men and women they have detained?

Countrymen, the corruption of the members of this neo-colonialist clique is notorious.

As I told you before, certain officers of the Police Service and members of the so-called National Liberation Council were involved in diamond corruption and when they realised that I had become aware of their corrupt and criminal connections with the diamond smuggling racket and that measures against them were imminent, they readily sold themselves to the imperialist neo-colonialists and conspired with them to stage the rebellion. They could only achieve their purpose with the aid of the army; and thus they conspired with the corrupt and morally weak elements in the army like Kotoka and Afrifa in order to achieve their treasonable objectives.

By playing stooges to the imperialists and the neo-colonialists, these corrupt army and police officers sought to escape the consequences of their crimes.

Countrymen, the crimes of the so-called National Liberation Council are many and heinous; and the misery, suffering and humiliation which they have brought upon the Ghanaian masses are immense. Several thousands of innocent Ghanaian citizens have been arbitrarily thrown into detention and imprisonment without trial and are all being held to ransom. All forms of social and political freedom have been suppressed by these renegades and hirelings of neo-colonialism. In fact, many of the letters I am receiving from Ghana are so cautiously written that one can even feel the fear of police censorship. It is for you, the masses, the workers and farmers of Ghana, both men and women, to rise up en masse and correct the many evils created by this notorious "National Liberation Council." You have the power to save Ghana and the Ghanaians from their misdeeds. As I have always assured you, the traitors of the so-called National Liberation Council and their hirelings may now suppress you with their tommy-guns and rifles, but in the final analysis, true political power lies solely with you, the masses. Do not be cowed or deterred by threats and victimisation for all these are only temporary. Soon they will all pass away and we shall have our free and beautiful Ghana with us again.

Men and women of Ghana, workers, farmers and peasants of Ghana, activists of the Convention People's Party, the People's Socialist Party of Ghana with all its associate wings, and the youth of Ghana, I call upon you to arise in your thousands. You have a duty to yourselves and your children; you have a duty to your country and to the African Revolution; you have a duty to the freedom fighters of Africa; you have a duty to liberate our dear country from the strangulating clutches of neo-colonialism and its hired stooges and lackeys. Arise, overthrow the so-called National Liberation Council and place Ghana, once again, on the socialist road to true independence, progress and prosperity. Arise and put Ghana back in the proud ranks of the African Revolutionary struggle. Arise and continue to make Ghana one of the pivots for the total emancipation and the political unification of our continent.

I know that you are faced with rifles, guns and bayonets and that it is somewhat difficult to organise either to demonstrate or go on strike without reprisals. But, as I told you in one of my broadcasts to you, there are many ways of killing a cat. You remember, in the pre-independence days of our struggle against colonialism we introduced sit-down strikes, either at home or at work. That is to say we either didn't go to work or we went and sat in the office and did nothing. You can apply this method to throw out these renegades, quislings and lackeys of neo-colonialism. You can apply this "sit-down-strike" in the offices, factories, workshops and even in the state farms. You are being suppressed and humiliated and any means at your disposal must be used to crush this notorious Ankrah-Kotoka-Harley neo-colonialist clique. Their wickedness, brutality and high-handedness, brutality and sadism must be brought to an end by all means. They are destroying Ghana financially, economically and ideologically. This Ankrah-Kotoka-Harley clique has been bought to do this and they are shamelessly and unpatriotically doing it without compunction. Unemployment is mounting high every day in Ghana. The rank and file of the unemployed is increasing daily. Workers of state enterprises have been thrown into the streets without work. The few at work are not being paid regularly. Some have their payments held up for months. This is due to the corruption and mismanagement of these idiots of darkness. The so-called National Liberation Council is taking steps to dismiss the directors and the management of the various state enterprises, corporations and factories. They intend to hand over the enterprises to private interests. They are anti-workers. The workers of Ghana should not allow this treachery to happen. You have a right to take over and run these state enterprises, corporations and factories yourselves. At any rate this was the basis of our work and happiness programme. And so by your taking over these state enterprises you are continuing the implementation of the Convention People's Party's Programme of Work and Happiness.

I call upon all the workers of each corporation, state enterprise and factory to oppose the handing over of the State Corporations to private interests.

You might as well take over these industries and run them yourselves thereby saving our state-owned industries from the clutches of neo-colonialism.

When a people rise against oppression, brutality and betrayal, they must do so without fear. After all, the peoples' revolution against oppression and misrule is made and won by the contest against odds. Therefore, people of Ghana awake! Arise and strike and destroy the neo-colonialist lackeys. The disgrace and humiliation which the so-called National Liberation Council has brought upon Ghana must be wiped out. It is only the men and women of Ghana who can do this. You made the revolution which saved Ghana from colonialism and you can save Ghana from this counter-revolutionary rebellion by the neo-colonialist quislings. Strike now and save Ghana! You can do it and you must do it. Sit in your homes or if at work refuse to work. Many of you have now become unemployed and many more are in daily danger of becoming so. But in whatever you do, remember that I am coming very soon. Those who have been thrown out of work and those whose jobs have been taken away from them will again be employed to work and serve Ghana. Those who may suffer victimisation must also have courage for they will be fully reinstated and compensated. This does not only apply to workers and farmers. It applies equally to the loyal officers and men of my armed forces and police.

Men and women of Ghana wake up and act; your once beautiful Ghana, with its world prestige and reputation, dignity and honour is being degraded and destroyed by these rascally agents of neo-colonialism. Everything in Ghana is now on a backward and downward trend. The national life and also your own individual lives have all been thrown into confusion, chaos and instability. The Ghana you counted stable is being destroyed before your very eyes. The so-called National Liberation Council have turned Ghana into another 'Gold Coast'. But remember there is no fortress, however formidable, that a united and determined people cannot overcome. Tommy-guns, rifles, and bayonets may temporarily put fear in you but they cannot destroy the spirit of the Ghana nation and its people. History gives enough evidence to prove this.

Remember also that in the face of oppression and misrule, the masses have nowhere to retreat and hide. They have only one battle cry. Advance and crush the oppressors! It is even humiliating to sit down and listen to the stupid and illiterate statements and the nonsensical effusions that come on Ghana Radio. How can you sit down there and watch our national newspapers degenerating into perverted gutter journalism? Even the news on our radio and television are insults to the intelligence of the Ghanaian people and their friends. The statements and speeches I hear on the Ghana Radio can only come from morons and idiots. They are not even a bad copy of their neo-colonialist masters' voice.

Men and women of Ghana, whatever the obstacles, whatever the oppression, brutality and vandalism, whatever the lies and false propaganda, whatever the neo-colonialist intrigues, arise in your mass strength and clean Ghana of this clique created by the intrigues of imperialist, neo-colonialism!

Now is the hour to strike, now is the hour to demonstrate, now is the hour to show that you are Ghanaians, wise and fearless. There is victory for us. Forward ever, Backward never.

Long live Socialist Ghana and her people

Long live the Convention People's Party—the People's Socialist Party

Long live the workers and people of Ghana

Long live the freedom fighters of Africa

Long live the African Revolutionary Struggle

Long live the Continental Union Government of Africa

13. The situation in Ghana has only sharpened the issues involved in the African revolutionary struggle, and increased the enthusiasm and consciousness of African revolutionaries all over the continent. . . . They (neo-colonialists) have fanned the flame of their own destruction.

12th June 1966

CHIEFS and people, men and women of Ghana, fellow Ghanaians, comrades and friends, once again I speak to you from Conakry on Radio Guinea's "Voice of the Revolution."

A week ago this Sunday, it was not possible for me to speak to you. I was then on an inspection tour of Guinea with Brother-President Sékou Touré. I visited several places and I was fascinated to see many of Guinea's development projects and plans, agricultural and industrial. I was specially interested to see the Kinkon Dam, a 3,200 kilowatts hydro-electric station at Pita. This project is very reminiscent of the 12 small sized dams, excluding the Bui Dam, which my government contemplated for Ghana and had surveys made of them. These plans have been halted and sabotaged by the traitorous activities of the Harley-Kotoka-Ankrah imperialist, neo-colonialist clique. These marionettes of neo-colonialism are bent on impeding Ghana's progress. But I am confident that in the very near future we shall be able to resume our task of national reconstruction and development without the sabotage, the obstruction and the impediment of external and internal reactionary forces and agents. The stooges and hirelings of imperialism and neo-colonialism must be brought to bay.

Friends and comrades, this Sunday, 12th of June, is the 17th Anniversary of the Convention People's Party. I know that because tommy-guns and rifles are being pointed at you, you are not able to celebrate this important political day with the public political rallies and merriment which have always marked this important occasion. Instead, you are being forced to listen to silly lies and stupid propaganda coming from your radio and television stations. I know that even though you are forced to hide behind closed doors and drawn curtains on this great day, you will be listening to me from your low-tuned wireless sets in the privacy of your rooms. I take the opportunity to salute you. I wish Party members and activists every success in your fight against the stooges and enemies of our country's development and progress. To those of you who are held in prison and also to those who, even though they are outside the prison walls, cannot celebrate this great day I say to you, take heart, the day of redemption approaches.

On that eventful day, 12th June 1949, I quoted you some words which I repeat to you now again so that those of us living can find consolation in them, and those who have died their names will be immortalised in the annals of Ghana's history as the simple men in whom Ghana's strength was ordained:

> "In all political struggles there come rare moments hard to distinguish but fatal to let slip when all must be set upon a hazard and out of the simple man is ordained strength."

Countrymen of Ghana, the problems and contradictions now besetting Ghana as a result of the irresponsible activities of the so-called National Liberation Council are many and calamitous. You all know how this clique of ignorant and self-seeking renegades have closed down most of our state-owned factories, corporations and enterprises thereby heart-lessly throwing thousands of workers into the streets, penni-less, without work and deprived of their livelihood or the means for sustaining their families. These traitors have set aside my Educational Programme for Ghana and are system-atically abolishing the free educational system which I and my government and the dynamic Convention People's Party worked so hard to establish. Under this our educational system, education was free from elementary to University level, text books were free for elementary and secondary schools, and elementary education was compulsory. Now this irresponsible Harley-Kotoka-Ankrah clique have threatened to abolish this system. I wonder how these ignorant traitors and lackeys expect the thousands of workers they have thrown out of employment and the hundreds of our Ghanaian women traders who now can't work, to get the means and wherewithal to pay school fees and buy text books for their children in the next academic year! To make the plight of these victimised workers even worse, the cost of living in Ghana is rising steadily daily—hunger and misery staring everyone in the face. Scholarship students at home and abroad have been deprived of their scholarships. Such are the tragic confusion, contradictions and hardships which now beset Ghanaians everywhere. But, the awakened workers of Ghana are aware and conscious of these hardships and contradictions and no amount of trickery and chicanery nor the useless creation of so-called "unemployment commissioners" can ever fool them. The fact that the notorious "National Liberation Council" is setting up unemployment commissioners shows clearly the depth of the degradation and deprivation which they have brought upon the workers of Ghana. Those of you who have made up your minds to emigrate from Ghana to other countries because of the criminal activities of the so-called National Liberation Council should not do so. Don't leave Ghana. Try and remain where you are for the so-called National Liberation Council and all that it stands for shall soon pass away.

Fellow Ghanaians, as I always point out, the neo-colonialist so-called National Liberation Council have been put there by their neo-colonialist masters to sabotage and destroy the socialist development of Ghana and also to attack and obstruct the African revolutionary struggle for total continental emancipation and unity. It is significant that in their treasonous rebellion one of the first objectives of the neo-colonialist Notorious Liars Council was to attack the African Affairs Centre and the Bureau of African Affairs which catered for African freedom fighters granted political asylum in Ghana. These traitors and stooges of neo-colonialism plundered the offices of these revolutionary centres and subjected the freedom fighters to the most inhuman treatment and humiliation, arrested them arbitrarily and then heartlessly carted away most of them to some gruesome fate at the hands of those from whom they escaped and sought political asylum. I learn that even as I speak to you now, some of these African Freedom Fighters are languishing in so-called "protective custody" while the traitors and imperialist, neo-colonialist quislings are secretly and quietly carting them away to a certain violent end. I salute these unfortunate Freedom Fghters and I pay homage to them. Let us always remember that the ~~
of the African revolution are immortal. I ~~
African Freedom Fighters and the many

ments engaged in the African Revolutionary struggle, for the unequivocal support they are giving Ghana at this hour of her trial. The new African is already awakened and fully conscious of the issues at hand. The giant continent is more than equal to any trial or imperialist, neo-colonialist intrigue and machination.

On 6th March 1957, Ghana victoriously won her independence from colonial rule and shook the imperialist world by promptly declaring her uncompromising stand for total African unity and emancipation. Since then our enemies have spared no effort to sabotage, subvert and discredit progressive Ghana in a vicious attempt to encourage their baseless contention that Africans are incapable of governing themselves. Thus they hoped to reinforce their feeble grounds for the continued exploitation of oppressed Africa. Of course our enemies failed miserably. Not only did the subsequent years see a train of newly-independent African nations which now number 36, but also the African Revolutionary struggle continues to liberate others still under colonial or settler rule in Africa. Pan-Africanism with its revolutionary struggle has come to stay and the goal set for a united Africa is irreversible. In 1963 the Organisation of African Unity was born in Addis Ababa and consolidated itself in Cairo in 1964. A further major milestone in the unremitting march towards the political unification of Africa reached its apex in the Conference of Organisation of African Unity held in Accra in October 1965.

Fellow activists of the African Revolutionary Movement, Freedom Fighters of Africa, the enemies of the African Revolution have always feared African unity and solidarity epitomised in the Organisation of African Unity. They have always sought ways and means to sow seeds of dissension and confusion among member states of the Organisation of African Unity so as to reduce its effectiveness and thereby obstruct the African Revolutionary Movement. Already they have concocted and are circulating ugly rumours about the October O.A.U. Conference in Accra last year. But, as Pan-Africanism continues to gain momentum, so the neo-colonialists and imperialists are losing political ground in Africa. Political independence without economic independence is meaningless. Hence also the struggle for Africa's economic emancipation. This struggle is perhaps more important and certainly more difficult than the political struggle. Its successful conclusion will usher in the final elimination of all forms of imperialist and neo-colonialist exploitation in Africa and the restoration of African dignity and personality under one federated Union Government for all Africa.

In Ghana, our Volta River Project, a hydro-electric complex, placed us on the threshold of a new industrial and agricultural era which guaranteed us real economic independence after years of unremitting hard work and selfless sacrifices by the people of Ghana. This is why the neo-colonialist, imperialists and their hirelings, lackeys and quislings consider Ghana to be too dangerous an example of African achievement to be allowed to continue under a progressive leadership. Our enemies see Ghana as one of the fountains of Africa's socialist ideological centres and a life-line in the African revolutionary movement. That is why they seek to destroy Ghana and her leadership. They seek to extinguish the fire of economic freedom which we have kindled in Ghana before it blazes throughout the continent of Africa. But the fire is already blazing in the cities, towns and villages of Africa. Even her forests and mountain tops are blazing hot. Africa is already awakened and fully conscious of the issues at hand. The imperialist and neo-colonialist clique in Ghana today, may cart away African Freedom Fighters to martyrdom but the situation in Ghana has only sharpened the issues involved in the African Revolutionary struggle and increased the enthusiasm and consciousness of African revolutionaries all over the continent. Indeed, by instigating the rebellion in Ghana our enemies have sown their own dissolution and doom. In fact they have fanned the flame of their own destruction.

The question then arises: Where do the Freedom Fighters and the African Liberation Movements stand in this phase of the struggle against imperialism, colonialism and neo-colonialism? There can now be only one answer. We have reached the final battlefield against the forces of imperialism and their neo-colonialist stooges and lackeys. The battle must now be fought to the finish and it must be fought with uncompromising zeal. Remember, our ultimate goal is one Union Government for all Africa. It is the only hope for Africa. It is the only road to salvation. Our contention is simple, clear and just. Africa is an indivisible whole. As now balkanised by artificial boundaries and fashionable imperialist, neo-colonialist doctrines, Africa cannot possibly come into her own. Africa must come face to face with imperialism, neo-colonialism and racialism. The hour has come to do so by the invincible revolutionary forces of Pan-Africanism.

In Ghana itself, the Ghanaians now know that Ghana is forever out of the gambling den of colonialism and neo-colonialism. Ghanaians will never allow themselves to be dragged back into that den again. They may now be forced to succumb to arbitrary rule by decrees, backed by tommy-guns and bayonets but soon they will rise to crush their criminal tormentors. Indeed the people of Ghana will be shocked when they come to know the number of people, men, women and children, whom the traitorous Harley-Kotoka-Ankrah clique have murdered in Ghana since their treasonable rebellion. It is interesting to note that the American Ambassador in Ghana is reliably reported to have described that dastardly rebellion as being—and I quote—"the most civilised coup" in living memory, meaning that the rebellion was bloodless. During the late February incidents in Ghana, that American Ambassador was present in Accra, and if he had been even a little observant and sincere, he could have seen the many lorry-loads of dead bodies of those killed by the Ankrah-Kotoka-Harley so-called National Liberation Council and buried in the Achimota forests and on the Accra beaches. Even the most "blind" observer is aware of the cold-blooded murder of Major-General Barwah. How can such a cold-blooded and ruthless massacre be described as a "most civilised coup?" It is unfortunate that the originator of this dishonest statement should have been an Afro-American. But perhaps he is either a corrupt hypocrite or an Uncle-Tom race-seller.

People of Ghana, men and women, activists of the dynamic Convention People's Party, these are difficult and trying days for you and I congratulate you for your gallant stand in the face of so many odds. I know the ordeals, the sufferings and the humiliations you are going through, and I also know the extent of the ignominy which the idiotic Harley-Kotoka-Ankrah clique has brought upon you. They seek to cover their treason and blind you by all sorts of silly lies and stupid propaganda. Our radio and T.V. have now been converted into media for propagating cheap propaganda and calumny. Our newspapers are muzzled and editors are forced to write lies and untruths. The neo-colonialist traitors are even using Flagstaff House to portray their perfidy by concocting lies and engineering staged performances calculated to vilify my person. But you the masses, know better and are aware of the facts and their reason for doing so. Stand firm, be steadfast and remember that whatever your sufferings and humiliation may be now, these are only temporary. You are not alone in this struggle. The mass constitutional forces inside and outside Ghana are all behind you. Be steadfast and stand ready to play your active part wherever you are. The hour of redemption draws near. Arise and gather inspiration from one another. There is victory for us. Forward ever, Backward never.

Long live the people of Ghana
Long live the Convention People's Party
Long live the African Revolutionary Movement
Long live the Continental Union Government of Africa
Long live Pan-Africanism
Long live the Freedom Fighters of Africa

And now, people of Ghana, men women and children, activists of the dynamic Convention People's Party, I charge you to rise and sing the battle hymn of the C.P.P., that hymn which inspired you to overthrow colonialism and should now inspire you to overthrow the neo-colonialist "National Liberation Council":

"Lead kindly light amid the encircling gloom."

14. I am, and still remain, the constitutional Head of State and President of the Republic of Ghana. . . . . I will be with you again.

5th December 1966

FELLOW countrymen, Chiefs and people, men and women of Ghana, fellow Ghanaians, comrades and friends, once again I am speaking to you from Conakry, where I have been living since I last spoke to you. This broadcast therefore comes to you from Radio Guinea's "Voice of the Revolution." My best wishes and greetings to you all.

Fellow countrymen, you have been told that I have resigned my constitutional position as President of the Republic of Ghana. *THIS IS NOT TRUE*. Let me repeat, *THIS IS NOT TRUE*. It is a calculated lie deliberately invented by the "N.L.C.," that Notorious Liars Council, to deceive my unfailing supporters, the Chiefs and people of Ghana. Such a lie only shows the depths to which these stupid, notorious liars have sunk.

Don't listen to them. Continue your resistance. All workers and others who have been dismissed, and those who are about to be dismissed, will all be reinstated in their various jobs as soon as I return.

I am, and still remain, the constitutional Head of State and President of the Republic of Ghana.

I am fit and well. I will be with you *again*. It won't be long *now*.

> Down with imperialism and neo-colonialism
> Long live the Chiefs and people of Ghana
> Long live the toiling masses of Africa
> Long live the African revolution

15. Stand firm and organise. Continue your resistance wherever you are. I have faith in you.

22nd December 1966

FELLOW countrymen, Chiefs and people, comrades and friends. Christmas is here with us again. I am speaking to you, in the spirit of the season, from Conakry, over Radio Guinea's "Voice of the Revolution." In spite of your suffering and humiliation I wish that you could have a merry Christmas and a Happy New Year.

This is normally a festive occasion. But on this year's Christmas Day, Ghanaians cannot help reflecting what a fateful year this has been for them. You have seen an unfortunate and sordid chapter in our history. It is a chapter of treachery and betrayal, of greed and hypocrisy, of cant and blunder. These are dark days in Ghana.

It is exactly ten months since certain officers in the Ghana Army and Police turned their guns at the very constitution and legal government which they solemnly swore on their honour to protect and defend. You know that anyone who is capable of such an outrageous betrayal of trust, for no reason at all, could never have been motivated by the true interests of the people. Events in Ghana since then, have confirmed this beyond any doubt.

Within ten short months the traitors who make up the so-called National Liberation Council have shown that it was their morbid lust for money and power, and their desire to escape from the just consequences of their corruption and crimes which made them commit such despicable acts of treason against the state and the people of Ghana. When you look around yourselves their only achievement has been the sordid reversal of Ghana's development and progress.

In these ten months a lot of lying propaganda and calumny has been manufactured by the so-called National Liberation Council. You have also been told a lot of nonsense by this Notorious Liars Council about the state of Ghana's economy. Far from the gloomy picture of doom which the so-called National Liberation Council have been at pains to paint in order to deceive you, there has never been anything like the

71

present state of mass unemployment and hunger which the last ten months of "National Liberation Council" misrule and mismanagement have brought upon Ghana. Thousands have been forcibly dismissed, or laid-off from their jobs. Mass unemployment has mounted so high to a stage unprecedented in our history. Let the unemployed therefore mobilise themselves and fight for their rights. Under me, all workers received their pay regularly and all state enterprises and organisations functioned normally and satisfactorily. In fact, ten short months ago the standard of living in Ghana was one of the highest in Africa.

What is the position today? Ghana's standard of living has fallen drastically. The cost of living has gone unthinkably high. Ghana's foreign reserves have entirely disappeared. The value of Ghana's currency has fallen hopelessly. In one of my broadcasts to you from here I warned that the opening of Ghana's borders, if not planned carefully, would lead to economic troubles. Today, Ghana's cocoa is being smuggled to neighbouring countries with disastrous consequences for the people of Ghana. Cocoa, the life centre of Ghana's economy, is in jeopardy, all because of the stupidity of the Notorious Liars Council and their ill-meaning advisers. Ghana is now in a mess economically and politically under the so-called National Liberation Council.

Men and women of Ghana, I know your troubles. Stand firm and organise. Continue your resistance wherever you are. I have faith in you. We have not fought so far and achieved so much only for us to stand looking unconcerned while a clique of deceivers and self-seekers do all in their power to turn the clock back. We shall not sit idle to see your hard-fought-for achievements being destroyed by this traitorous clique before your very eyes.

The so-called National Liberation Council have become infamous for their brazen lies. But, by telling you that I have resigned my constitutional position as the President of the Republic of Ghana, even they, the Notorious Liars Council, have outreached themselves. They have indeed demonstrated to the world the depths to which they have sunk. In my last broadcast I told you that this was *not* true. Let me say it again today that that is *not* true. I have *not* resigned my position to anybody; it is a characteristic lie which has been deliberately

72

invented by the Notorious Liars Council to deceive all those millions of you who remain loyal to me.

Fellow Countrymen, on my return all workers who have been dismissed will be reinstated. Free medical care and hospitalisation will be restored. Education will once again be free at all levels and text books will again be supplied free of charge. All scholarships of students both at home and overseas which the so-called National Liberation Council have withdrawn will all be reinstated. All Ghana state properties and enterprises which have been handed over to foreign firms and individuals by the so-called National Liberation Council will be restored to the state. To all those Ghanaians who have suffered untold injustice from the so-called National Liberation Council's misdirected and prejudicial commissions of enquiry, justice will be done. The Chiefs who are suffering now will have immediate justice done to them.

Fellow Countrymen, in celebrating this year's Christmas, let us remember those who have been murdered by the so-called National Liberation Council in our struggle against the marauding dangers of neo--colonialism. Let us also spare a thought for those who are suffering in detention camps and prisons in Ghana today. They will be released on my return to Ghana.

Don't despair. I bring you a message of hope. I wish you all good health. Take heart. I will be with you again. It won't be long. There is victory for us.

> Long live the Chiefs and people of Ghana
> Long live the workers of Ghana and Africa
> Long live the African Revolution
> Down with imperialism and neo-colonialism

CPSIA information can be obtained
at www.ICGtesting.com
Printed in the USA
BVHW070717240519
549224BV00002B/115/P